Discover, Reflect & Connect
with Words That Can Transform Your Life

CHARITA H. CADENHEAD

1 WORD

Published by Purposely Created Publishing Group™

Copyright © 2017 Charita H. Cadenhead

ALL RIGHTS RESERVED.

No part of this book may be reproduced, distributed or transmitted in any form by any means, graphics, electronics, or mechanical, including photocopy, recording, taping, or by any information storage or retrieval system, without permission in writing from the publisher, except in the case of reprints in the context of reviews, quotes, or references.

DISCLAIMER: Although each author may have conducted some research in order to support their writing, this book is in no way a compilation of scholastic research.

Printed in the United States of America

ISBN (ebook): 978-1-945558-19-1

ISBN (paperback): 978-1-945558-18-4

Special discounts are available on bulk quantity purchases by book clubs, associations and special interest groups.
For details email: sales@publishyourgift.com
or call (888) 949-6228.

For information logon to:
www.PublishYourGift.com

DEDICATION

This book is in loving memory of my Grandmothers:

Ruth Ware (Ruth Ma), whose words I could always count on to make me laugh;

&

Ann Carthan (Ann Ma), who always had an encouraging word.

◈ CONTENTS ◈

Acknowledgments			xi
Preface			xiii
Chapter 1:	Trust	Sreelatha Meleth	1
Chapter 2:	Imagine	Carole Hines-Sharp	9
Chapter 3:	Resilience	D. Green Joseph	17
Chapter 4:	Brave	Sabrina Mays	27
Chapter 5:	Destiny	Patricia A. Campbell	35
Chapter 6:	Faith	Lupe Moreno	43
Chapter 7:	Listen	Hermione Alease Carnes	53
Chapter 8:	Home	Brenda Mullen	67
Chapter 9:	Curves	Aimee Lanier-Camper	75
Chapter 10:	Stillness	Donna T. Brown	85
Chapter 11:	Believe	Timekia Brayboy	95
Chapter 12:	Impact	G. Michelle Hale	103
Chapter 13:	Intentional	Brandy Bonner	111
Chapter 14:	Hope	Charita H. Cadenhead	121
1 Word Book II			135
Your 1 Word Journal You			137
About the Authors			145
Sources			159

◇ ACKNOWLEDGEMENTS ◇

I would like to personally thank every author that contributed to this book. Each of you jumped on board without hesitation. When I launched the call for coauthors, some of you I had known for years, and others I had never laid eyes on, which was really amazing to me. My friends and acquaintances knew they wanted to be a part of this because of who I am. Then there were the authors who trusted me sight unseen and never a word spoken, yet you climbed on board the *1 Word* train.

I extend my thanks to all who supported and encouraged this project verbally and in silence.

I would be remiss if I did not acknowledge you for purchasing and reading this book. Ultimately, the goal is to have you walk away braver and more hopeful, faithful, intentional, trusting, impactful, and understanding of your destiny. If we have been successful in conveying the significance of our one word, then you will now be able to identify the one word that has found a home in your heart and mind, despite the curves of life, and you'll learn to listen to your word with great anticipation of something wonderful occurring. As a result, you'll be B.R.A.V.E enough to accept any

1 Word

challenge that I you face and know that resilience is a part of your D.N.A.

◈ PREFACE ◈

As far back as I can remember, I have been fascinated with the way people communicate. Particularly, I am interested in their word choices and whether they use words in the way that they actually intend. Or are their word choices simply chosen at random merely out of habit?

My decision to write this book came from a situation at church involving a spiritual analysis that I had taken. The analysis caused me to rethink my position on the word hope and come to grips with a truth that may have been apparent to everyone except for me.

The more I thought about this word *hope*, I wondered if people, like yourself, have an attachment to a particular word, and if so, could you talk or, in this case, write about a single word and answer the following questions?

- What does the word mean to you?
- How does the word make you feel?
- What was a turning point when you had to apply this word to your specific situation?
- How did or does the word move you from where you were into how it serves you now?

1 Word

This wasn't an easy project for some of us because in many cases, we only thought we knew how our one word impacted us. To some degree, it turned out to be an experiment that caused us to examine how words play out in each of our lives. During the course of writing, something magnificent happened with each keystroke. We discovered something new about ourselves. Some of this new information was good and some was not so good.

Ultimately, it was the discussion of our one word that caused us to think about how words affect us in a general sense. But to effectively communicate the power of our word, we had to whittle our focus down to the much narrower scope that shined a light on the words that we speak to ourselves and the words that resonate with us the most. That being said, it may not be easy for you to identify the direct influence of a solitary word. You too may discover what you thought you already knew.

How to Read and Use this Book

The idea for this book is to rediscover the meaning and power of words that go beyond superficial usage and application.

A clear example of rediscovery is an example I heard Joel Osteen use as I watched him one Sunday morning. He reminded us of the old adage, "Sticks and stones may break my bones, but words can never hurt me." As if we didn't know how hurtful words can be, Osteen gave us a stern reminder that words can, do, and will hurt. He went on to say with tremendous emphasis how untrue that statement is, and that we should even stop teaching our kids that words don't hurt. Words often become thoughtless clichés, with no real connection to present situations, like the Osteen example. They are often used out of habit rather than truth.

This book is designed to send you on a quest for internal truth and depth while reinforcing the need for self-reflection that encourages and motivates rather than disguises, deceives, and destroys. I suggest that you have a dictionary handy because as you seek to discover your own set or subset of impactful words, a refresher course might be in order, much like needing to retake elementary algebra before moving on to a higher level of mathematics. I can guarantee that once your mind starts ticking, you'll want confirmation and clarification on what you once thought was perfectly clear. You may be surprised to discover that you've long forgotten the true definition of words that frequently flow from your lips.

1 Word

While the authors have written about their selected impact word, we want you to take time to reflect and consider how their one word may have or have had a sweeping impression in your life. If not the writer's one word, then one word of your own choosing that is perhaps a constant or reoccurring presence in your psyche.

As you read this book, read it like you can hear the writer thinking their thoughts out loud as they are writing in their journal or merely having a moment of self-reflection. It's important to read each chapter that way in the beginning, so you'll know how to frame your own thought process in preparation to analyze the significance factor of the word in your life.

Don't be in a hurry to read the book or get through it quickly. Take some time in the process—as long as you need—to sit quietly and uninterrupted so you are able to contemplate and absorb the connotation of the one word. Acknowledge any feelings or thoughts that you are having about the focus word. Answer the questions above and the ones that each author poses in their chapter and determine how you will use that word to make a difference in your life and the lives of others.

In so reading, consider that the words you speak to yourself can either lift you up or tear you down.

Acknowledge which applies to you. If it is negative, let this book and the time you spend with yourself be your motivation to turn the negative into a positive. Use the power of words to speak life over yourself and the people that you love and care about. Use it to communicate with people in a way that may not be the norm for you.

Create your own list of words that significantly impact your life in the way that you think, make decisions, and get motivated, or perhaps make a list of words that tailspin you into despair or devastation. Let words wander freely in your mind.

By harnessing the power of words, or even a single word, you can better understand where your strengths and weaknesses are drawn from and make adjustments where necessary. Don't let change scare you into inaction, but rather let it catapult you into action.

Before you begin, review the questions again to help you understand what the authors have been asked to consider about their one word. The overarching purpose of this book is to get you to do the same.

Trust

SREELATHA MELETH

When I decided to participate in this book, I prayed and meditated on the word that I should be learning and writing about. The first word that floated into my mind was *trust*— not trust in another person or even myself. It was trust in the sense of faith in the goodness of life.

Life Is Happening for You

Tony Robbins says, "Life is not happening to you, it is happening for you." How many of us can say that we truly live in a space where we trust that life is indeed happening for us? I know for certain that I cannot. We pray, and we say that we believe in God, but almost as soon as we get up off our prayer seat, our minds race off to the situation that is dominating our thoughts at the moment. There have been several instances of this in my life. Each time we worry, regardless of the circumstance that is causing the concern, whether it is about our work, children, health, finances, or the next terrorist attack, we are announcing our lack of trust in life.

You win the battle with distrust at all levels when you can settle into that knowledge that life is happening for you. Once you move into that space, it does not matter much whether you trust other people or yourself; you live with a foundation of trust that lets you know that in the long run, there are no mistakes. There is a plan, there is a path that you are meant to tread in the world, and there is a loving and graceful force that makes sure you go down the path you are meant to. The incredible fact about life and God is that opportunities to rest in the peace never stop coming to us. Every moment of every day is a choice to choose trust or fear.

Trust the Process

Some of my most vivid memories of making the choice between trust or fear are from the six years my family spent in the United Kingdom. My husband was in the process of getting his post-graduate training in clinical medicine, which meant that he was on the lookout for a new job every six months to a year. Given how busy he was, I was the person who scoured the vacant positions ads in the *British Medical Journal* and sent out his resume to thirty or forty hospitals around the country. This was in the early eighties, so I could not rely on Google. For each application I filled out, I found the place where we might live on a map, tried to read up about it, and became excited or worried about the possibility.

After I would send the applications out, I would spend weeks, sometimes months, tight and wound up inside. Every time the mailman came, my heart was in my mouth. Each day that passed without a response added to the stress, and I would go up a notch on the worry scale. What if none of the hospitals respond fast enough? What if we are left in this foreign place without a job? We have two children; how will we manage? What will people back home think about us?

I lived out the shame and worry of that circumstance every day, so at a certain point, it became too stressful to carry the burden. It was as if my insides had gotten so tightly twisted in a knot that there was nothing to do but unravel. Grace intervened, and a small voice inside me started saying, "It will be fine." My breath got a little deeper, my stomach less clenched. The repeated playing of doomsday scenes in my head got fewer and further apart.

Without fail, I had a magical day when I was finally able to let go completely and allow the "It will be fine" mantra to take over my spirit. Invariably, it was only when I got to this place of trust that we would hear back from a hospital. It was often just one hospital that responded to us from the thirty to forty applications that went out—but one did. It was as if there was a hand leading us on the exact route we needed to take through the array of available NHS hospitals to prepare my husband for his exams. There was a plan. I did not know it, but as I look back now, it was clear that there was a path we were meant to walk. All we (I) needed to do was to trust that it was there.

Although my spiritual practice was not as stable and solid as it is today, I recognized each time this happened that I was being taught a lesson in trust. I was being shown how letting go and resting back allowed me to understand at some deep level that life was indeed always unfolding in my favor.

Trust, Tragedy, Triumph

Our trust is threatened the most when the very foundations of our lives are rocked with an unexpected tragic death, a fatal disease, or an unexpected betrayal. We feel unhinged, as if we are no longer able to stay in our bodies.

Trust includes knowing that stuff often hits the fan and that life goes on, even when it feels as if the very foundations of your life have been shaken. How can you talk about trusting life, you may ask, when we have just witnessed a horrendous spree of events like the shooting in Orlando, the senseless murder in Nice or Istanbul or Baghdad, or the mass shootings in Newtown or Columbine?

The fact is that it is also important to recognize that the very same events, the most frightful and unbearable without exception, also provide opportunities for us to experience the full splendor and generosity of the human spirit. These are experiences that we would not have if it were not for the horrible tragedy that gave rise to it. The Schindlers, the Wintons, the Gandhis, the Martin Luther King Jrs., and the Nelson Mandelas of the world would not exist if it were not for the horrible atrocities perpetrated by the Holocaust, colonialism, racism, and apartheid.

Does the fact that the most horrific and awe-inspiring actions coexist in the same moment in time take away the horror of the event? No! But it does show us that we are so focused on the horror that we often have no time or energy to take in the other side. The simultaneous coexistence of these two categories of action continually reinforces the eternal duality of our existence. Light and dark, bone-crushing anxiety and inner peace, fear and valor, and joy and despair all live side by side. It is impossible to experience the joy and peace of one without having known the sorrow and fear caused by the other.

In a certain sense, it might be easy to make sense of such events when there is some distance between us and the victims. It is so much harder to maintain trust when you go through an experience that feels as if the structure of your life is coming apart. Mouthing platitudes, such as "Everything happens for the best," is hardly helpful to a person who is going through devastating heartbreak. In that instance, trust is holding that person in their pain, allowing and validating that moment in their life as real. If you face heartbreak head on, you will hopefully see that one of life's biggest gifts is that it is relentless.

You think that after something devastating happens, life must not or cannot go on, but it does. The next day comes and then another. Incredibly, in spite of what can only be described as soul-crushing sadness, one is still breathing, feeling, eating, and drinking. Part of trust is allowing life to unfold as it will—feeling everything and resisting nothing. It may be impossible for the person who is experiencing the shock to feel this trust. Our role in that space is to not let the foundations of our trust be shaken as well. Our role is to dig deep and find that space where we know that allowing our loved one to fully experience the pain will not make them disintegrate. It is about resting in the knowledge that nothing happens in our life that we are not able to face. It is understanding that at times, in order for us to be put back on the right path in life, we get knocked on the head with a two-by-four or stabbed in the gut. Despite all of that, life's saving grace is that it goes on.

Putting Trust to the Test

The truth of the matter is that as I write this, I am struggling to find this trust. It almost seems as if the due dates for this chapter were planned to make my experience of trust even deeper. Life has thrown an unexpected curve ball, and I have been struggling to rest back into trust.

Everything that I have written about above has been asked of me. I am being asked to trust life while near and dear ones experience despair. I am learning what it feels like to hold the space for them and allow life to happen. I have understood that it

1 Word

is possible for me to expand my energy, become stable in my energy field, and then hold friends and family who are experiencing bone-crushing anxiety and soul-crushing loss, without being pulled into it myself.

I have learned that it is possible for me to change and impact how others feel, regardless of the physical distance between us. I have also learned that this building of trust is a work of constant practice. It is something that I have to constantly go back to and rebuild in myself from one moment to the next.

This is a very different me that is going through this experience. An earlier version of me would allow the terror, fear, and worry to take over. Not this time though. This time, I am allowing life instead of resisting it and running in circles to push away the experience. I am amazed and grateful that my spiritual practice over the years has brought me to a place where I am more and more able to embody the knowledge that I can trust life.

I am trusting.

I am letting go.

I am resting back.

I am relaxing in the flow of life, knowing that it is always unfolding in our favor.

Imagine

CAROLE HINES–SHARP

Simple. Empowering. Symbolic of eloquence, deliverance, and destiny. Infinite.

As I began to ponder which word to write about, I took some time to think about the message that I wanted to convey about my word. I wanted a word that represented infinite possibilities; a word that is shaped by our own desires and is only limited by one's self. I sought out a word with intuition. And trust me—this was not an easy task because in my deliverance, it was important to me that my word would touch the very soul of its meaning. I myself had to feel good about the word and how my deliverance would impact and make you feel.

As I pondered for weeks over this word, I began to imagine. I wanted this to be an interactive process, so I asked myself, how can I deliver a message so meaningful and have my reader involved in this process? It seemed like a real challenge at the time, until I myself started to imagine. I began to imagine in my own mind what it was that I wanted to say and how I wanted you to perceive what I had to say. And my word was breathed into this chapter. My word is *imagine!*

Let the Journey Begin

To be a part of this journey, start by taking a deep breath. Reach into the stratosphere of your mind and envision your life as it is "supposed to be." Go deeper. Take a couple more deep breaths and go deeper. Relax. Close your eyes. Are you there? Where did your imagination take you? Are you fulfilled? Were there failures? Situations that you wish you could have handled differently? Disappointment? And what about the "what ifs"? We all have the "what ifs" and the "shoulda-coulda's" in our lives, right? To help me, I'm going to ask you to stop and make a list of goals that you wish you could have accomplished. Take your time and be true to yourself.

All done? Great! Now I'm going to ask you to reach into the deepest part of your imagination. Where are you? How did you get there? Where do you want to be at this very moment? You see, the beauty of (our) imagination is that it brings you to a place of hope and belief. It allows us to dream. What if your life was put on hold due to life's circumstances? Were there disappointments? Did you give up? Now close your eyes again and imagine being in that place. What is stopping you at this very moment? Can you imagine accomplishing those goals? Being in that place? Fulfill your dreams by imagining yourself there. The possibilities are endless.

Now imagine just one word that defines who you are and what you would like to accomplish. Write a short paragraph defining a simple goal. Imagine yourself accomplishing that goal. Then, write down your word. The mind is very powerful, and we all have attainable goals if we allow ourselves to imagine being in that place.

Imagination Kicks into High Gear

In October of 2012, I was diagnosed with breast cancer. Aside from my mother, husband, and children, the first person that I called was my cousin Patricia Jackson, affectionately called Patty. Very powerful in her faith and conviction, Patty said to me, "I hope it is not triple negative breast cancer." Now, I had never heard of the term triple negative breast cancer, and until then, I just thought that breast cancer was breast cancer. I had no idea that there were different types. I just heard of the various stages. But a couple days later, I called Patty back and said yes, it is triple negative breast cancer.

By then, I had been educated and knew that it was an aggressive type of breast cancer, and that I very well may be in the fight of my life. When I called Patty back, her words of usual encouragement were, it's okay, we are not going to worry about it; we are going to pray about it. God bless her soul. At that very moment, I had to imagine life without me in it. What was I going to do? Of course, when you hear those dreaded words—you have cancer!—your imagination takes you into so many emotions and scenarios. I kept thinking over and over, what am I going to do? Am I going to die? Am I going to live?

I had so many emotions and tears, and of course, I felt sorry for myself. Imagine the look on my mother's face while trying to be strong for me, her only child. Imagine the tears that I shared with my husband. My family and closest friends were full of emotion. Imagine telling your children and grandchildren and not having the answers. Imagine not being able to tell your daughter who is away at college because she is taking finals, and you know it would affect her greatly. Imagine that!

Get a Grip

I thought back to a cold day in January 2009 while in Washington, DC, at the inauguration of our first black president, Barack Obama. I was so captivated by the words of his inaugural speech as he delivered with resilience, "Starting today, we must pick ourselves up, dust ourselves off, and begin the work." Those words became a staple in my home: pick yourself up, dust yourself off! And that was exactly what I had to do. And once I picked myself up and dusted myself off, I began to imagine myself living! I knew that I had work to do. And when I began to *imagine* myself cancer free, I began to believe. To dream. We have all had those pick-yourself-up times in our lives when we may have faced setbacks. The challenge becomes answering the question, where can my imagination take me?

When I was asked to write a chapter in this book, I knew the possibilities were endless. But where would I start? Not ever having undertaken a project of this magnitude, I was excited by the opportunity, but apprehensive about how I would be perceived as a writer. Could I deliver the message? As I began to allow my imagination to be free, I felt more and more challenged to use my

1 Word

own imagination, just as I have asked you to be a part of this project in envisioning and imagining your own dreams.

Okay, Now It's Your Turn

Now I am going to ask you to deliver. You began by imagining where you wanted to be, realizing missed opportunities. Essentially, I asked you to face whatever obstacles are impeding your most inner possibilities. I asked you to do that by imagining. When you went deep into your imagination, how did you feel? Did you realize the endless opportunities? How did your imagination make you feel? Did you feel good? *Imagine* is not only a word, but it is also an emotion.

Now, I want you to make another list. This time, list your accomplishments. Write how you feel about your accomplishments. We all feel good when things are going well, right? It is equally important to recognize your accomplishments and your dreams fulfilled. Stop and write down your accomplishments and speak to how you are fulfilled because you have realized these dreams.

Now I am going to ask you to compare the two. Take a moment. Close your eyes again and envision your first wish list, so to speak. Now, envision those goals realized. Can you write about how you feel about both of these lists and imagine how one relates to the other?

You see, sometimes what we perceive as missed opportunities are actually obstacles. But if you can envision those obstacles as opportunities and set your imagination free, you come to realize that "a door closed is a door opened" is not cliché if you can imagine where you want to be and what you want to do. Imagine yourself in that space.

Once, I imagined myself in a world post–breast cancer diagnosis. Post chemo, post radiation, post hair loss. Everything was post, post, post. But then I began to do what I asked you to do; I closed my eyes and began to imagine I was set free. I imagined that I was healed and cancer free. I imagined that I would live a long and fulfilled life. I imagined that I would see my children and grandchildren grow into productive adults. I imagined that I would see my daughter graduate from college. Lastly, I imagined that one day I would write a book. In that book, I would be able to have an impact on someone's goals and dreams by empowering them to imagine and believe them into existence.

When I close my eyes, as I have asked you to do, the possibilities are infinite, and I feel so empowered. Empowered that my dreams can and have become realities; empowered that I have

1 Word

imagined my dreams into existence; empowered that I believe in you, and that if you will allow your imagination to run wild, you will be so empowered to imagine into existence.

So now that I have given you the foundation for my choice of words, how can you be so empowered? How can your imagination, or lack thereof, define your destiny? Did our interactive process give you the opportunity see yourself differently? Perhaps some of us have had to forgive ourselves to move forward in being who and where we want to be. Perhaps we have had to forgive others to move forward as well. I imagined myself being a better person, and who doesn't feel good about that? I also imagined myself being an advocate for other women diagnosed with breast cancer, and I have imagined it into existence.

Because you have made the decision to imagine into existence, how does it feel? What steps will you take? Perhaps you imagine yourself as an author, a better friend, an advocate for the poor, or a student. The possibilities are endless when you imagine. Will you hold yourself accountable?

Earlier, I asked you to write down one word to describe who you are. Open your eyes and imagine. Are you that person? Why?

Resilience

D. GREEN JOSEPH

If there was ever one word that encompasses power and strength and weakness and vulnerability at the same time, it is resilience.

It seems that feelings of helplessness, downtroddenness, and despair exist in order for resilience to come to the rescue.

Resilience: What Is It?

To be resilient, you must have experienced an event or circumstance that had a seriously adverse affect, causing you to bounce back or recover. Wouldn't you agree? Webster's Dictionary defines resilience as "the ability to become strong, healthy, or successful again after something bad happens,"

1 Word

and "the ability to return to an original shape or state after being pulled, stretched, pressed, bent, etc."

Another description of resilience, from wisdomcommons.org, states that it "is rooted in a tenacity of spirit—a determination to embrace all that makes life worth living even in the face of overwhelming odds. When we have a clear sense of identity and purpose, we are more resilient, because we can hold fast to our vision of a better future." I really like this description, but I realize that a "clear sense of identity and purpose" are not always present when one is faced with a difficult situation.

Now that this power-filled word has been defined and explained by others, let me express my feelings toward this word *resilience*. This word provides me with a sense of empowerment and edifies hope. Who among us hasn't suffered challenges? Truth be told, all of us have. Challenges may vary in size, weight, and intensity, but they are still challenges nonetheless. To be truly resilient indicates that you can take a licking and keep on ticking. It means that for some reason, you have been down but not out! It infers that you have been the beneficiary of unforeseen and often unpleasant circumstances only to survive and emerge better and stronger. Can you feel the power this word holds?

Childlike Resilience

I find it interesting that the word resilience is often used to describe children. There is something to be said about having a childlike outlook and resolve. In Matthew 18:3 KJV, the scripture says, "And said, Verily I say unto you, Except ye be converted, and become as little children, ye shall not enter into the kingdom of heaven."

Children tend to view things in a far simpler way than adults. Isn't it amazing how in our youth, we felt like there was nothing we couldn't do or survive? In our minds, all things were possible, and we shrugged at the thought of anything knocking us down or slowing us up. Adulthood brought about new realities and understandings, some of which robbed us of our hope and optimism. But I believe in spite of many of life's challenges, within all of us, there is a get-back-on-track fortitude that surfaces and props us up until we are able to take back the wheel and steer the car of life back onto the road.

Activating Resilience

What causes you to activate your resiliency? There are many reasons to be resilient. Here are examples of situations to consider that may cause you to rely on the ability to be resilient:

1 Word

- Loss (loved ones, peace, stability, relationships, jobs, income, divorce, material possessions)
- Repeated and consistent disappointment
- Despair (hopelessness, depression)
- Defeat (business, job, unfulfilled dreams)
- Steady stream of bad news and bad fortune
- Lack of finances
- Love

The last bullet is the most important to me. My child caused me to kick my resilience into high gear! Both love and loss catapulted me into a place of uncertainty, sadness, and insecurity. After the death of my husband and best friend, I was left a thirty-eight-year-old widow with a fourteen-year-old daughter to raise alone. My initial grieving period was short-lived because my main concern was for her. I wouldn't allow myself to completely fall apart. For me, the loss itself was enough to move me from sorrow to a state just short of full-blown depression and insanity, but because of my daughter, I allowed resilience to show up and do what it does best: nudge me into taking that first step away from the cliff of my emotions. To have stayed in that state of mourning would have been selfish and self-destructive, so resiliency placed my daughter in its cross hairs and provided me the focus needed to inch back from just existing to living again.

Sometimes it is someone versus something that causes us to put ourselves aside to ensure their wellbeing—resiliency for the sake of love. It wasn't until I lost my parents and my husband that I began to fully gain a deeper understanding of the legitimacy of resiliency. Resilience is an unselfish word. It never stands alone and tends to attach itself to something (a situation or circumstance) or someone (friend, family member, or lover). When something or someone changes, usually in a negative way, we are often affected negatively, but at some point, if allowed, resilience shows up.

The Punching Bag Effect

In *Life, the Truth, and Being Free,* Steve Marboli says, "Life doesn't get easier or more forgiving; we get stronger and more resilient." No truer words have ever been spoken! Life is no cakewalk, at least not for most of us. I am about to disclose my age now—do you remember the inflatable punching bags that some of us played with years ago? It seemed that no matter how hard we punched, it never failed to pop right back up. It swayed, wobbled, and even turned around, but never did it fall.

That reminds me of the resilient person: when life throws a punch, we stagger, kneel, bow, lean, tilt, sway, and even sit, but once we are renewed, we get back up and return to our original position. Battle scars, scrapes, and bumps are sometimes visible, but I believe they exist as a temporary reminder of what we have been through. During the healing process, scars and pain subside, and new skin replaces old wounds. Resilience after a battle!

Mind, Body, and Resiliency

Resilience is as much physical as it is mental and spiritual. The Bible states in Ephesians 4:23, "And be renewed in the spirit of your mind." Because the mind, body, and spirit are all interconnected, each part should experience a portion of resiliency in order to be balanced. When we seek clarity, understanding, and peace in the midst of adversity or confusion, I believe this represents resilience for the sake of balance and comfort!

"No matter how you define success, you will need to be resilient, empowered, authentic and limber to get there," writes Joanie Connell in *Flying Without a Helicopter: How to Prepare Young People for Work and Life*. According to this quote, in all aspects of life, including work, there is a need for resiliency. How interesting! I propose that in addition to teaching math, science, art, and technology, we also incorporate lessons for our children in activating resilience in order to be truly successful.

The thing about being resilient is if it is not a constant, active, existing part of your being, you can and will become consumed by the issues that have the potential to impair you long term. I liken this state of being consumed to drowning. For those who swim and those who don't, I know all of you have had an encounter (good or bad) with a pool or body of water. Be you a seasoned swimmer or beginner, the first experience of sinking to the bottom of a pool is terrifying!

You can only hold your breath for so long before panic begins to take over. As you open your eyes and focus on the surface above, where the freedom to breathe resides, you regain some composure, but the challenge still remains—how do you get to that place where water and air meet? Here's how: with persistence, effort, and deliberate, strong, strokes of arms and feet, you push your way back to your original point of entry, and BOOM—resilience for survival! When you harness a can-do spirit, resiliency is invoked! Sometimes sheer stubbornness is the driving force that bridges the gap between reluctance and a resilient resolve.

1 Word

Resilience and Me

Resilience also means to continue, never-ending; it has action and motion attached to it. Resiliency is a state of being. When I think of being resilient, I think of moving from one state of being to another. The vehicle that carries me from one state to another is resilience. This word can be as powerful as a tidal wave, or it can be as simple as a single footstep. Resilience means overcoming, pressing forward, shifting slightly, or perhaps taking a giant leap, so it definitely involves change!

When I utter the word *resilience,* I immediately feel a sense of power and pride. Why pride? Because history is full of examples of resilience. The Bible is full of narratives about people who faced great challenges and sometimes even major defeats, but most were able to bounce back. In every human category imaginable—from the millionaire to the single father, from the president to the homeless—there are people who allowed resilience to take hold and do its job. The word resilience makes me realize how strong I am, and the proof is reflected in the mirror.

The Turning Point

Simply stated, the turning point for me, when resilience played a role in my life, was through love and placing someone else's best interests above my own. Now that I consider most challenges to be mere bumps in the road, and I have stopped viewing them through a magnifying glass, resiliency shows up much more quickly. Thanks to my changed perception, the need for it is not as often. Where I was once an oak tree that would uproot whenever a storm hit, I am now a palm tree—I bend, bow, and hold my ground. I am not uprooted.

Your Turn—How Does Resilience Influence You?

I now have a much better understanding of exactly how resilience directly and indirectly plays a vital role in my life and the lives of the people connected to me. Now that we have examined and explained the word *resilience,* when you think of this word, what comes to mind? What life memory or experience do you connect resilience to?

The English language contains an estimated 1,025,110 words, so I encourage you to stop and take just a moment to think and make a list of words that resonate with you. Then narrow that list down to one word that speaks to you the loudest. Explore it, talk about it, write about it, embrace it, and most importantly, share it!

Brave

SABRINA MAYS

You get one opportunity in life to be who you are going to be, so ask yourself these questions: How many people can be number one? How many people can be you? This book is titled *1 Word,* and we have a choice every day to be representative of one of the words highlighted in this book.

Who Am I?

My mom named me Sabrina, but God whispered in my ear and told me my name is Brave. Bear with me for a while, and you'll see why He gave me that name and why I cherish it. I have faced a wide array of opposition on this journey called life;

however, I have learned that opposition creates an opportunity to show why God named me Brave.

At first, I doubted everything about my God-given name. I would wake up in the morning looking for excuses as to why I could not be brave. I would look at people who I considered affluent and instantly put them down, simply because in my mind they had made it. They were brave enough to allow their ideas, dreams, or visions to work for them. Whose fault was it that I hadn't made my dreams a reality? Who was I to blame? After all, God doesn't make mistakes, so who was I to blame for not being brave enough to make it? Furthermore, what does it mean to have made it anyway?

There are countless days in my life when He has revealed to me that I am brave, and I finally got it. I had it all wrong. I am brave—not in the sense of being courageous, but rather in the meaning of this acronym: Be Resilient, Add Value Every day. I had to learn to see myself as God sees me, which meant that I would have to stop looking to people to validate me, lift me up, or embrace the ideas that God had given me. I trademarked them with God's stamp of approval, and no one can carry out these ideas like me because no one can be me.

What I See in the Mirror

One day, I looked in the mirror, and I absolutely hated everything about me. I looked at my life and thought I had failed in every aspect. I had failed as a Christian, wife, daughter, mother, sister, and friend. I even failed as an enemy because I can't hate people. Nothing in my blood permits me to hate them. I began to wonder what the world would be like without me. I wondered what difference I would make in this world. I began to seriously believe I was no good for anyone or anything.

When these toxic beliefs started to take up permanent residence in my mind, God stepped in and sent me two signs from two of the most peculiar people. I say peculiar because out of all of the people I know, these two are the most unlikely to volunteer advice without first being asked.

What Others See in Me

One Sunday, I went to church as usual. When I came home I took a nap, not because I was tired, but because I didn't feel like dealing with my reality. I didn't feel like being a Christian, mother, daughter, sister, or friend. I didn't feel like being at all. If life were a fairy tale or cartoon, I would have made myself invisible or waved my wand

1 Word

and whisked myself away to some magical place. However, no matter how brave I may be, that is not possible. When I awakened, I knew I had to still deal with it all.

The buzzing sound of my cell phone vibrating did something it had never done before: it woke me up! There was a text on my phone from a guy—not just any guy, but one from my past. He's married now, and we are distant friends, but we both realize that we learned a lot about life from one another when we were together. As a result, every blue moon, he reaches out to me just to talk. On this particular day, the text message was different. It read, "Just listen . . . Powerful," with a link attached. I clicked the link, and it was a gospel song by John P. Kee, "Wave It Away." There was a second text, which read, "One thing I have always admired about you is you're a winner, and my thoughts of how you push through gets me through some of my worst days." I listened to the words of the song: "I am the victor. I can conquer anything." These words were the very essence of my name, Brave. The song went on to say, "I cast my cares at your feet." Well that got me to feeling some kind of way. I can't say it motivated me, but it got me thinking.

I recalled the message from the sermon earlier that day. God will send you a message from the most unlikely places, but you better be ready and open to listen and receive the message. I got up from the sofa and said, "Stop feeling like a loser, you can do this!" I continued to go about my day, but when it was time to go to sleep that night, I couldn't. I was all over the place. My mind wasn't clear. I read article after article, watched YouTube channels, and even took a green tea bath. Nothing seemed to help.

Around 1:00 a.m., I sent a text to a guy I secretly loved. In the text, I mentioned not being able to sleep. Now he would typically send a provocative response, but this time, he sent me a text with a link attached that said, "This is my go-to inspiration." Well guys, that did it! My first thought was, this is weird. God, are you trying to tell me something? I clicked on the YouTube link (https://goo.gl/CHigZW), and it was life changing. The speaker began by saying, "You can be brave enough to write every one of your goals down, but life is going to hit you in your mouth, but get back up because your WHY has to be greater than the knock down."

After listening to the hour-long speech, I couldn't sleep! I was on fire. I thought about my why. Why do I keep going? Why do I get back up? Why can't

1 Word

I just stay down? Why does any of this even matter? The answer was simple but true. God said, that's how I made you. The guy sent me a second text, which said, "If this doesn't make you feel like you can conquer the world, then you are a pussy . . . quit being a pussy!"

Brave Catapults into Action

That week was rolling! I put plays into action. I was crossing out items on my to-do list left and right. Then by midweek, that little voice of doubt started to seep in, but he wasn't about to win. I had to travel to another state toward the end of the week. While driving, a thought came to mind: you've been knocked down on your face so much, they should call you flathead, but you get up and twist it off because you're not the typical screwdriver. You are built tough! In that moment, I realized why God gave me the name Brave. He equipped me to be brave. He equipped me to face adversity by trusting Him.

Through obstacles, I have learned that as long as I trust Him, be resilient, and never give up, He will give me the strength to keep going and add value every day. It's not just about adding value to all you do, but adding value to the people you meet. He shows me I'm worth it. All the obstacles that may appear as failures are actually triumphs to Him because you keep going. Trust He knows what is best for you. Your failures can't compare to your faith.

You are unstoppable because God has your back. If you just remain brave, every day will be a day worth living. Every day belongs to Him to have His way with you. If you remove yourself from the equation, He moves inside of you.

I Hereby Appoint You Brave

When you think of someone who is brave, who do you think of? You probably think of warriors, heroes, and courageous individuals. God said, "Girl, that's how I see you! Don't let the world trick you. I have something in store for you. You don't need approval from the world when I told you I got you. You don't need to be appointed by man when you are anointed by me. They can't take you where I can. They can't love you like I do. They cannot dictate to you who you need to be. I created you exactly the way I wanted you to be. I just need you to trust me. Do you trust me?" He asked, "Can you do it? Are you brave?"

Those were three simple questions I had to answer. All of them determine my fate. What will determine yours? Will you be B.R.A.V.E. enough to walk the line even if you have to walk alone?

1 Word

Will you be B.R.A.V.E. enough to listen even when you don't want to, or if the message comes from some unlikely place? Will you be brave enough to push yourself to be the best you that you can possibly be, even if no one is cheering you on? Tell me this—how many people can be number one? How many people can be you?

God told me, "When I changed your name, I changed your identity, so walk with authority. It takes a mighty person to be brave. It takes courage to be who I have called you to be." We only get one opportunity to be who we are going to be in this life. I choose to **B**e **R**esilient and **A**dd **V**alue **E**very day. What about you? Can you be resilient and add value every day? How? Why or why not?

Destiny

PATRICIA A. CAMPBELL

One word can change your life. My life-changing word is *destiny.* So what does it mean? Destiny is a predetermined course of events considered as something beyond human power or control (freedictionary.com). The scripture supports this concept in Jeremiah 29:11 NLT: "'For I know the plans I have for you,' says the Lord. 'They are plans for good and not for disaster, to give you a future and a hope.'"

In Search of Destiny

Knowing that my creator had a plan for me encouraged me to seek my plan. But like many others before me, I did it in an unorthodox way!

1 Word

Growing up in the sixties and seventies, I did it my way, which led to many unsuccessful trials. Intuitively, I knew that there was something special I was to do, but I could not put my hand on it. I was sure of one thing: in order to walk into your destiny, you must leave your comfort zone.

Leaving your comfort zone can be pretty scary. As humans, we are not comfortable with the unknown. It is very easy to get stuck in a rut and just glide through life aimlessly. During the process of discovering your destiny, you will experience setbacks, missteps, and discouragement. Always keep in mind that our God is monitoring your steps, and if you listen closely, He will guide you to your purposefully designed place.

I have discovered that destiny is a process, and some people find it sooner than others. Life is not about finding yourself; it is about discovering who God created you to be. When you are born, you appear to have a blank slate, but a strategic design for your life is imbedded deep into your DNA. This discovery begins with the first breath—you know, when the doctor spanks that bottom, and you let out that loud cry!

Destiny: Yours, not Theirs

As you began to grow and develop, you probably

heard people say, oh, you look like a teacher, or you are going to be a nurse, doctor, engineer, pastor, poet, and on and on. Accepting as fact the suggestions of others is one of those places that you can get stuck in making everyone happy but you. Sometimes our parents and well-meaning friends, relatives, or even teachers see greatness in you, but they want to live vicariously through you. You end up on a life track that pleases everyone but you. You have succeeded at pleasing everyone and doing well, but you don't feel fulfilled.

On the flip side, people say mean things that do not encourage you to achieve. This negativity can cause you to get all the way off track. Below are ways to overcome negativity and stay on track:

1. Set your vision.

2. Focus on your vision.

3. Rehearse your vision.

4. Expect your vision to manifest.

In the process of life, you will be presented with many opportunities to fail or succeed. Be careful to always seek wisdom to choose the right path suitable for you. If you listen to your inner self, it will gently guide you to your divine purpose, which is your destiny.

1 Word

That Moment of Clarity

Allow me to share with you an opportunity that was presented to me. One evening, I attended a speaking event at the Alabama Theater. I didn't have a clue who the speaker was or what in the world I had gotten myself into. The place was crowded, so I sat there and began to look around. I thought to myself, I don't see a band, the movie screen isn't down, and there are no trailers running. I was just plain stumped!

Finally, a rather nice looking man came up and took the mic. He said, "Hello, my name is Les Brown." He engaged me with conversation, motivation, exhortation, and even laughter. Through this motivational conversation, Les Brown touched the very fabric of my mind, will, emotion, imagination, and intellect. He transformed my forgotten dreams and visions that life had long ago buried, and he brought those dreams back to life. Wow, it was like Jesus calling Lazarus from the grave! Needless to say, I experienced a powerful and explosive night! After that motivational moment, my life changed. I came out of my comfort zone and began to explore my dreams and visions, one by one. I began to come up with innovative ways to make them happen. This same experience is waiting for you! Start listening to your inner self today. Once providence provides you with that initial catalyst, you are on your way to realizing your destiny. You will find yourself walking out of your comfort zone. As humans, we are not comfortable with the unknown. Destiny is doing what you are created to do.

Yes, I was already a productive citizen, but I was not totally fulfilled. I did not own my entire God-given power. Your personal power comes when you live your destiny. That day in the Alabama Theater, I realized that my heart had to change. Something was keeping me from moving forward. Les Brown encouraged me to look into my heart and discover what was in it. He encouraged me to perform a kind of spring cleaning of the heart.

After that compelling presentation, I reluctantly looked into this old heart and discovered some things that were in dire need of being discarded. You must go through this process before you can activate your word properly. In my heart, I found things like anger, fear, strife, envy, jealousy, forgiveness, bitterness, pride, insecurity, and procrastination. Wow, this was a major discovery!

The Process

You can mask what is in your heart, but the fragrance of an unhealthy heart shows up in various ways; stagnation is just one way. You must face the fact that you have a contaminated heart, and for real growth to begin, you must purge your festered heart. To rid myself of my heart condition, I had to submit to surgery. This was not a natural operation but a spiritual one. I was in need of a spiritual heart transplant.

As I sought my heavenly Father for guidance, I realized that I had to ask Him for forgiveness for being slothful and inattentive to my prescribed walk. Life and unfortunate circumstances caused me to harbor these feelings. He forgave me for harboring the negative emotions in my heart and allowing these emotions to hinder me and keep me from experiencing the plan He had for me. After forgiving me, He gave me the strength to forgive myself for the many mistakes that I made innocently as well as intentionally. He gave me a new heart—one filled with love, joy, peace, happiness, and determination.

With my new heart, I could clearly hear the strategy for my next move: education. What school should I attend? Ironically, I received an invitation to a recruitment event at a local college. The timing of this request seemed divine! Naturally, I agreed to attend. I was so impressed with the presentations at the college recruitment event that I felt compelled to become a student—right then and there. So here I was, a mother, working a full-time job, and caring for an ailing parent. Nevertheless, I was inspired to become a student again.

Now, this journey was not a simple one, but with my new heart and my divine strategy, I moved forward! To attend college required adjustments in my lifestyle as well as the lifestyle of my family. I did the research and found the appropriate college schedule that met my needs. The additional finances fell into place. When you are walking out your destiny, life has a way of providing the very assistance that you need. My experience in college was an outstanding one. I made many new friends and developed many new skills, and one could say that I expanded my horizons!

The word destiny came alive in me. It caused me to search deep into my inner self. To still my heart so that I could hear the word, the one word, that I was searching for that would ignite the fire in my life. Destiny caused me to grow and expand my mind, intellect, emotions and imagination. Life is not about finding yourself; it is about finding who you were created to be.

Through a series of events, this one word made me a better person. Discovering this word destiny and applying it to my life prepared me as a college graduate to serve my family, community, and government with the spirit of excellence. This journey began, as I stated earlier, with soul searching. As the master planner unveiled the essential strategies to me, I was willing to adapt my life to His plan. When you are born, you appear to have a blank slate, and reaching your destiny is like a rhythm that you march to and maintain. The quest to find God's dream for you is your destiny.

This quest is called the process of life, so no matter how winding the road, destiny is achievable through faith, obedience, and a submitted will. Destiny is a series of events that must transpire to get you to a certain place.

Faith

LUPE MORENO

What is faith? The American Heritage College Dictionary defines faith as "a confident belief in the truth, value, or trustworthiness of a person, an idea, or a thing; belief that does not rest on logical proof or material evidence; loyalty to a person or thing; and allegiance." It is also defined as "a secure belief in God and a trusting acceptance of God's will." In the Bible, Hebrews 11:1 ESV describes faith as "the assurance of things hoped for, the conviction of things not seen."

Before I began to write this chapter, to me, faith meant having a very strong trust that everything is working out and going according to God's plan, whether we like what that plan is or not. However, as I began to pay more attention to my daily life, I began to see how it is also important to have faith in others as well as ourselves.

Faith Is a State of Mind

A part of having faith is your state of mind. During any situation, you can choose to think negatively or positively. This can be in regards to employment, relationships, school, travel, finances, etc. The law of attraction states that we attract what we think about. If you have faith in yourself that you will do well in a job interview, then chances are higher that you will do well. However, if you go in there thinking negatively and without confidence, then it will show, and that could affect whether or not you get the job. Have faith in yourself and know that you can accomplish anything you put your mind to. "I can do all things through Christ who strengthens me" (Philippians 4:13 NKJV).

Have you ever applied for a job that you knew you were qualified for and that you felt really good about when starting the interview, only to be turned down for the job? How did you feel when you were notified that you did not get the position? Were you disappointed in yourself? Did you feel inadequate or put yourself down? I used to think that way about myself, until I changed my mindset and started to have more faith that everything was working out according to God's plan for me.

You see, sometimes when we ask for something and we do not get it, it is because God has better plans for us. We may not realize it at the time, but it is true. In early 2012, I was applying for different jobs because I was no longer happy with my employer at the time. Although I loved the job itself, it had become a hostile work environment. I started to see a therapist because of depression and other side effects of PTSD (caused from my prior history of domestic violence). I was getting very discouraged. In the past, when I didn't get jobs that I had applied for, I always ended up getting a better job with better income and benefits. I kept reminding myself of that and kept thinking that there was a reason why I wasn't getting hired now.

I had to keep the faith that God had something better waiting for me. Within a couple of months, I was given the opportunity to start my own business. I knew without a doubt that this was why I wasn't being hired. I submitted my resignation and became an entrepreneur in June 2012. Being an entrepreneur opened many doors for me and provided me with many new opportunities, including being a coauthor of this book. From then on, I no longer got disappointed when I didn't get something I wanted. Instead, I started to thank God because although I did not know at the time what He had planned, I knew it was something better! I would say out loud, "Lord, I don't know what you have planned for me, but thank you for what you have coming!"

The next time you do not get a job that you applied for, or you do not get something else you have been wanting, do not get disappointed or beat yourself up about it. It is not because you were not good enough. Have faith that God has something different planned for you and give Him praise.

Praise God like Jehoshaphat did in 2 Chronicles 20. Praise and thank Him *before* you get what you asked for.

Faith and Relationships

This same sort of faith can be applied toward relationships. If you are in a bad relationship, or you are single and think that you won't ever have a truly happy marriage, change your mindset and start to have faith in God that He will send you your perfect spouse. You are worthy of happiness and love! You are worthy and deserving of someone who will love, honor, trust, and respect you! All you need to do is ask God and have faith that He will bring it to you.

I know because after being the victim of domestic violence for over twenty years, I began to lose faith that I would ever have a happy marriage. I started to give up on love and settle for relationships that did not give me the love, respect, and happiness that I deserved. I started to feel unworthy and ended up marrying a man who I was not in love with. It did not take me long to realize it was a mistake, and we filed for divorce about a year after the marriage. I was giving up and starting to think I would just stay single for the rest of my life. After all, it was better to be single and happy than to be in the wrong relationship and unhappy. That did not last long though.

One day, I decided to pray to God and tell him exactly what I was looking for in a husband. I was specific. I decided to stop looking for a relationship and just live my life one day at a time. When the time was right, God would send my new husband to me. Within a few months, God sent me my husband! We met one evening while I was out with a friend of mine, and we connected instantly. He was everything I had asked God for and more. After previously being victimized in two abusive relationships, followed by several other failed relationships, I finally knew what it meant to have true love! God gave me my heart's desire, but it did not come until I trusted in Him. "Therefore I say to you, whatever things you ask when you pray, believe that you receive *them*, and you will have *them*" (Mark 11:24).

Faith Is Mighty

Have you ever found yourself worrying about finances and not knowing how you are going to pay your bills? That can be a very scary and stressful situation to be in. It leads to sleepless nights and can affect your health. I know because I have been there! The worst time in my life, when I would say that I hit rock bottom, was in September of 2003. As the result of being involved in a financially abusive relationship, I found myself in a position where I no longer had a job; my bank account had been closed due to too many checks with insufficient funds; my credit cards were all maxed out and in collections; my car loan payment was months overdue; and I had been given a three-day notice to pay my rent or be evicted!

I was a single mom with three young children, aged ten, nine, and six. This was the turning point in my life that ultimately made my faith stronger and has affected my life ever since. After getting that three-day notice and not having any family or friends who could help me out, I knelt down on the side of my bed and cried out to God! I told Him that I needed His help more than ever before, and I needed Him to save me. I did not know how He was going to do it, but I knew in my heart that He had it under control. After praying, I felt this peace overcome me. Even though I knew God was going to fix it, I knew I also needed to do my part and take action. I got temporary financial assistance and food stamps, and I got some assistance from my church.

Within one month of getting down on my knees and praying, I had a job! Within two months of praying, I had been reinstated to my previous position as a management assistant with the county of Ventura in California. I once again had a well-paying job with full benefits. I once again had a bank account and had been approved for a new credit card to start rebuilding my credit. I was paying my bills, and God was restoring all that had been taken from me. He did not stop there, though! Six months later, I moved to a different job where I was given a 10 percent raise and even better benefits! Within one year of the day I prayed, my debts were all paid off, except for my car, but that was paid off soon after.

Since then, when things get rough financially or in any other way, I think back on that time and how God not only gave me back everything that had been taken from me, but He also gave me more! Compared to that, problems now do not mean too much because I know without a doubt that if God got me through that, then He will get me through anything! The next time you start to worry about finances and what you will do, trust that God has it under control. However, you also need to take action to find a job or brush up on your skills. God will open doors where they need to be opened.

Faith in People

Having faith in a person is trusting that they will do something and having confidence in them to carry it out. For instance, if you have ever had surgery, you needed to have faith that your surgeon had the proper training to operate on you and that they knew what they were doing, right? Worrying about a surgery and its outcome only causes more stress to your body and can affect your healing.

When flying on an airplane, you need to have faith that the pilot is trained to fly the plane and get you safely to your destination. If you worry and have anxiety on a flight, especially a longer flight, then you will miss the view of being above the clouds. Flying above the clouds is a beautiful experience! The clouds look like many cotton balls spread across the sky. While looking out the airplane window, you can also view the beautiful scenery down below and possibly see some beautiful sunsets and sunrises. Even during times of turbulence, have faith in the pilot to get you through it. When I travel on an airplane, and there is turbulence, I think of it as being on a roller coaster, and I just ride it out. I have faith not only in the pilot but also in God that He is protecting me. It's during times like these when we need to have faith even more; it takes away our worry and replaces it with peace. "Yea, though I walk through the valley of the shadow of death, I will fear no evil; for thou art with me; thy rod and thy staff they comfort me" (Psalm 23:4 KJV).

Faith: Have It. Keep It.

When we pray and ask God for something, it is our faith that will make miracles. The Bible tells us we only need to have faith the size of a mustard seed. If we pray but then doubt that our prayer will be answered, we are not really being faithful and cannot expect our prayer to be answered. Faith erases any doubt, worry, or fears that you may have and replaces them with comfort and peace. Faith can also replace sadness with happiness, feelings of rejection or unworthiness with gratitude, and feelings of despair with hope.

Having faith will also give you peace until you take your last breath. I witnessed this with my father before he went home to heaven. Even while he was on his deathbed dying with cancer, my father never lost his faith. He kept reading his Bible, praying, and worshiping God. When he could no longer read, my family took turns reading to him. We played praise and worship music for him to listen to when he could no longer sing. The night before he passed, he told my sister that he saw doves flying above his bed. He knew that he had fought the good fight, and he was going home to be with Jesus.

Faith gives me peace, joy, comfort, love, confidence, and gratitude. It has helped me through failed relationships, disappointments, health problems, financial issues, and overcoming my insecurities and low self-esteem. How you live your life from this moment forward is up to you to decide. You can live stressing about things, worrying, and being afraid, or you can choose to live in faith. I pray you choose faith.

As you can see from reading this chapter, faith is very important to me. It guides me in all areas of my life. How has my chosen word of faith influenced your own word?

Listen

HERMIONE ALEASE CARNES

Listen: "to pay attention; heed; obey; to wait attentively for a sound" (dictionary.com). This word is commonly used, yet everyone has a different perception of what it means. It is a verb; therefore, it necessitates action. Immediately, action sets one apart from everyone else. Many people don't like to take action. They would rather assume a passive role, let things happen, and follow someone else's lead. "Anyone can hear, but leaders listen" (*Active Listening,* ELMS.Aspira.org).

I have always been a listener, and I believe listening to others is of utmost importance. I am a woman of few spoken words. I am described

1 Word

as quiet, and at times, unconcerned. We live in a world where those who talk the most or holler the loudest reign supreme, but they often produce sounds of emptiness and ego. However, it is I, the listener, that is the most attentive—the most actively engaged and the most able to perceive situations more closely to the correct inference.

When I listen, I do so to gain understanding. A true understanding of a person, situation, or idea is often far more important than we would like to admit. Listening for understanding is what I hope you will do as you read this chapter. So grab a cup of coffee, your favorite pastry or comfort food, and listen with your heart as you read. As a Christian, chef, entrepreneur, and active family member and friend, listening to my instincts and listening to others is a constant balancing act. For this reason, I am driven to create positive and peaceful environments. I do this by carefully choosing the people who have access to me and by carefully and intentionally setting up my home and workspaces in such a way that they invoke an atmosphere of peace. Because prayer is an essential part of my life, I even carefully select times to pray and meditate in order to optimize my focus on the act of listening to God as he speaks to me.

Chef and Entrepreneur

Let's start with the obvious. As a chef, I love good food. My father taught me to cook when I was eight, and I have been cooking ever since. I used to watch him in the kitchen, and I would listen to all of the sounds he would make while cooking. Often, he would be singing. This most likely necessitated the need for me to listen to music—mostly gospel and jazz—while I work. By doing so, the kitchen becomes my sanctuary. If I am to listen to words while cooking, they must be uplifting, positive words. If the words do not create a positive atmosphere, I would rather have no words at all. If another chef I am working with brings negative energy into the kitchen or to a project, I can immediately sense the difference in the food and the atmosphere.

Hearing positive words allows me to tune into my inner voice (instinct) while working. When I am operating from a peaceful and positive place, my instincts will whisper to me "use thyme instead of oregano; this will give the dish a unique flavor," or "this client suffers with high blood pressure; you need to use more fresh garlic." You may say, Hermione, that doesn't make sense; you speak of hearing a voice in the kitchen while you cook. Precisely, I say, listening to my inner voice in the kitchen has made me the professional I am today.

My father encouraged me to obtain a business degree in accounting because I was strong in mathematics. After five years of college, I completed my degree and began working in the accounting field, all the while cooking for friends and family until my father's passing. Listening to my father's advice, in regard to my major, was a sage piece of advice for my life. In my profession, passion is more important than profit. There are many chefs that do not bother with or even know what a balance sheet or income statement is. Listening to my father, in this instance, gave me an advantage in culinary school and as a business owner. This is an example of listening to and following the right advice.

I started my catering service at the age of twenty-nine, the same year my father passed. Immediately after his death, what I listened to became confusing. Although twenty-nine is considered a very mature age, I did not have much experience making my own decisions. I was very naïve, so I listened to everybody. I thought everyone had my best interest at heart and wanted the best for me because I never wished any ill will on anyone else. I believed everyone in my inner circle (my family, my friends, my church, my schoolmates, and my coworkers) thought like me.

This was not only confusing but also dangerous. It was confusing because I valued everyone's opinion; therefore, I listened to everyone. It was dangerous because those who knew how naïve I was gave me advice to keep me off track or to keep me where they would be comfortable with my life. I did not believe I had a choice in deciding what was best for me. Eventually, because of the strong paternal presence in my life, I learned to trust my gut.

I had been working for BellSouth Telecommunications for over five years and catering on the side when I heard my inner voice whisper to me, "Quit your job." The voice gave specific instructions: cater full-time and register for culinary school. The voice I heard gave me Bible verses Hebrews 5:11–14 KJV. I wasn't completely sure about what to do, so I waited for six months. Then circumstances began to show me, in plain sight, that this instruction was definitely for me. I was extremely exhausted from working full time and catering, and I would fall asleep at work. I was very depressed about going to work. I also had this unremitting feeling deep down inside of me that I was created to do more in life than just work a nine to five job.

When I followed the instruction, the catering jobs increased in number, and the quality of clients increased as well. This increase was only for a season though because I had yet to understand the profit patterns of the catering industry. I became frightened, so I picked up several part-time jobs for about two years during this time of transition from gainfully employed to entrepreneur. This was a very insecure time in my life. I was trying out my wings, so to speak. I learned how to live on $100 a month and sometimes $3000 a month, not knowing what amount was going to manifest and when it was going to manifest. The one constant I found was that whatever amount I had, everything was always taken care of. I never went hungry; I was never in the dark or cold. I may have had only a fourth of a tank of gas, fifty cents in my purse, and an overdrawn bank account, but I was okay.

I learned from this lesson the importance of listening to my inner voice but also how to discern between the time when you must take action upon what you hear and when you should simply be still. I believe I should have researched my industry's peaks and valleys before I quit. I used my 401k proceeds to fund my business, but I did not manage them well because I did not prepare properly for the lean seasons.

I began to connect with people who possessed the same entrepreneurial spirit I possessed.

Through one of my first moves out of Alabama to Georgia, I connected with two ladies: one was a childhood friend, and the other was a young lady who was following the same path as me. In retrospect, I now know this was my first test of listening to my instincts. Both of the ladies were a blessing because they both taught me valuable lessons about what I should listen to. One did so with antagonistic words and interactions; the other with benevolent words and interactions. What I came to understand about each one was that one was operating from a false sense of security, while the other from an authentic security. Needless to say, at that time, I was not as strong in my faith.

The opposition seemed much louder and stronger than I, so I moved back to the security of Alabama. Upon my return, I connected with four seasoned entrepreneurs: two men and two ladies. From the two men, I learned the practical knowledge of doing business. The ladies provided words that continue to be a source of motivation. Their words reminded me of my worth, and I replay their statements over in my head when I need uplifting. After several trials, I transitioned from listening to my father's voice to listening to my own voice for over fifteen years now.

Mother, Daughter, Sister, Friend

1 Word

These four titles describe other areas of my life that I must master daily. You too may have the same titles and feel that they overwhelm you. I have to reiterate that listening is the principal thing, even in these multiple roles and relationships.

Whether we realize it or not, God places every personality type, weak or strong, loving or hurtful, inspiring or negative, into our family unit. These are the first people we learn to relate to: mother, father, sister, brother. God surrounds you with these people to shape and mold your destiny. As you grow, you begin to interact with aunts, uncles, cousins, grandparents, etc. These people are inevitably your life's framework, and from them, you learn how to make decisions about which friends to connect with, who to marry, which career to choose, etc. These are the first people you observe and listen to for advice. They shape the way we listen and what we listen to about ourselves.

My mother and father have always been positive voices in my life. My father called me "Bubbling Brown Sugar." He always told me, "No matter what, remember you are the grand prize." In reflection, these words of affirmation planted a seed. Of course, there are outside sources that come to destroy the seed: "You are too dark," "You are not shapely enough," "You are too insecure," and "Your parents spend money on your clothes because it makes you look better." For some reason, I listened to these voices in my younger years instead of remembering what my mother and father told me. These negative words made me feel bad about myself. They made me feel like because I couldn't change the way I looked, no matter how I dressed, I had no choice in the matter. To choose which opinions I listened to and which ones I ignored was not an option for me. I felt as if I had to accept everything that happened to me. This included the way others treated me. Now those opinions seem absurd and totally irrelevant to me.

The seeds of affirmation that my parents planted earlier in my life now ring loudly in my ear, and because they resonate in my spirit, I can easily differentiate what I should listen to for me and my son's life, and what is just simply noise or chatter. Please understand that some criticism is used as sandpaper to smooth out unstable areas of your life; therefore, you shouldn't avoid it altogether because you won't evolve into the person God has in mind. Everything that is beautiful and rosy is not always going to make you grow. Sounds disappointing, but it's true. This revelation comes with maturity.

1 Word

I have a friend that I often speak with over the telephone. I call him my voice of reason. My dad called him "an electric shit-talker." My dad was hilarious that way. Even though my friend and I only talk maybe three or four times a year, he has continuously been my biggest cheerleader. On those occasions when we talk, he always has encouraging words for me, and his words are always timely. As in all real friendships, we have our disagreements, and we sometimes stop speaking for a while—mostly when I am operating from a place of insecurity and fear when it comes to making decisions for my life. Everyone has to go through something that is challenging in their life. Those events usually teach you a lesson and equip you to teach others the lesson. My lesson is to listen and be fully present with people I love. Listening validates the speaker, and everyone wants to be valued.

My point here is that you should surround yourself with voices and words that speak life, truth, and love. These voices will

- Tell you what is best for your child.
- Instruct you on how to relate to your parents and siblings.

- Reveal to you who your true friends are and how much access each one may need to have to you.

- Tell you the reason for the connection and whether it is for a lifetime or a life lesson.

- Reveal to you when you need to be a true friend and cause you to tell a friend the truth, even if it means never speaking to them again.

Life is so fast paced, and decisions often have to be made in a millisecond. How can you listen when everyone and everything is bombarding you at once? Like me, you have to create a time and place to listen. Listen to what encourages you, to what gives you peace, to your inner voice.

Christian

After my father's death, I began to cultivate a deeper relationship with Christ. I began to study the word, fast, and pray for understanding of my purpose here on earth. With no self-confidence, and the depression from my father's sudden passing, I still felt in my gut (my instinct) that I was put here to do more, and that small voice that had been playing in my head all of my life made me stop, get still, listen, and search for clarity and truth. The seeds of affirmation that my parents planted earlier in my life began to ring loudly in my ears and resonate in my spirit because they aligned with what the word of God and my instincts were saying to me. I can now easily differentiate what I should listen to for me and what is just simply noise or chatter.

The key difference in hearing and listening is using your brain. The brain is connected to everything in your body, including your heart. Your heart is where your creator, Jesus Christ, should live. The inner voice that I speak about comes from Him. Your creator knows what is best for you. After all, He is the manufacturer of your existence. He knows why you were created, how long you have to complete your assignment, and which attributes and resources you will need to complete the assignment. He will give you warnings, encouragement, direction, and ability.

How do you listen? You listen in prayer, fasting, reading the Bible, listening to music, and dreaming. These activities authorize Christ to dwell in your heart. They silence the voices that tell you that you are not worthy; they replace the horrible memories of your past, even as far back as your childhood; they slowly get rid of all the hype that the world screams is truth and replace it with your designated truth, designed by your creator. Developing a relationship with Christ reveals who you are and the purpose for which you were created. Once you know in your heart these two things, you become invincible. Not that you are immortal, but you will know what you should listen to and what you should not listen to.

If what you hear does not agree with what is in your soul, it is not for you. I am in no way saying that if it feels good to you, then do it. You must first take the crucial journey to give Christ the first place in your life. He will become the advisor of that inner voice when this happens. He will give you clues, and He will allow you to make the choice to follow his advice or do otherwise.

When you listen to your inner voice, you make the intentional choice to hear God's best for your life. Truth, love, and power will direct your steps.

Home

BRENDA MULLEN

Home. This word has a myriad of meanings and can be used a variety of ways. It can be a noun to mean place of residence; it can be an adjective to describe something in sports, such as home base. We see the word everywhere. While sitting at my computer, I can look up at the top right of whatever web browser I'm using and see the word home, and I know clicking that button will take me to where I want to go, back to my home page on the web.

In conversation, the meaning of home is dependent upon the context in which it is used. Everyone knows what home means or is at that

1 Word

given moment; however, the word itself draws such an intimate feeling from most people. When one talks about home, the visions, thoughts, and feelings associated with that word are as different as there are types of people on the planet. It's also a word that evokes a ton of emotion. Just think of the song Home by Phillip Phillips. Once that song came out, it became a number one hit immediately. Why? Because it was a song that everyone related to in their own way.

For me, home makes me think of a refuge. It is not just a place to reside in or a button on a computer to take me there. It's a feeling I'm looking for, or to put it another way, that place that gives me a feeling of safety, of belonging, and of being able to be free to be myself without any pretense.

Home used to be a place that seemed elusive to me for much of my life. Now home is a part of my career in that I am a REALTOR®, and I help people find a home in the physical sense. But more importantly, I'm able to be a part of their journey to find that feeling of what home means to them.

The Search for Home

Looking for home seemed to be something my mother and I were always doing. I grew up in a single-parent household (my mother was married twice). My biological father, whom I never remember meeting in person, was a man given to drinking and hitting. My mom left him when I was just a baby. My stepfather was a marine, and my mother was only married to him for a short while; however, during that time, when I was around five years old, I lived in many different places, such as Athens, Greece, and Sudan, Africa.

My mother and stepfather ended up getting divorced when I was around seven. We were in California then, and it was around that time when I first started realizing my mom had a wanderer's heart. She never stayed in one place too long. During those earlier years, my mother and I lived in some interesting places, including a commune. Apparently, they were all the rage back then. I don't remember too much about the experience, except that is where I learned that I disliked powdered milk and tofu (horrible stuff if you ask me and nowhere to be found in my home now). I also lived with my grandmother for a while in Rochester, New York. Living with my grandmother felt a lot like home. It was nice that we were all together, and I could stay in one place.

When I was about ten years old, my mother decided to move us to Albuquerque, New Mexico, so we packed up and hit the road in her blue Buick

1 Word

Skylark. I believe that's where I get my just-do-it-and-see-if-it-all-works-out mentality—from my mother. It was quite an adventure driving from the East Coast to the West Coast. When we finally arrived, we had to live in a hotel room. Since my mom didn't have a job yet, it was touch and go until she could find work. She eventually found a job working as a security guard, and we were finally able to move into a one-room efficiency place downtown. I know she was happy to get out of the hotel room and have a place we could call our own, a home. I'm not sure that I ever felt at home there, but at the time, it was much better than a hotel room. We used to laugh and say you could brush your teeth, shower, and use the restroom all at the same time in our very tiny bathroom!

Thank goodness we did not stay there very long, as the area wasn't a terrific place to live. In fact, my mother and I moved twice more, and for some reason, it was always around Christmas. We would always pack up the Christmas tree and the presents, along with our belongings, and haul them all to a new place. Every time we did that, it was a bit funny and sad at the same time. Funny because hauling a decorated Christmas tree tied down to a truck was just silly looking. Sad because Christmas is a time when emotions are at their highest, and it seemed like we were always searching for but never really finding home, a place with lasting memories and emotions.

Could This Be It?

Around the time I was about to enter into high school, my mom was looking for another place to live. I was tired of moving and having to make new friends each and every time. I was always the new person, and I never got the chance to really fit in. There's always a bond between people who grow up together (much like the security of home), and that's something that I didn't have.

I asked my mom if we could stay in one place at least until I graduated. She promised that when we moved again, we would stay, and she kept her promise. Oddly enough, the day I graduated high school, I moved out on my own and into an apartment with friends. Being young, dumb, and the know-it-all that I was at the grand old age of seventeen, I moved back in with my mom within a few months.

Apparently, having my own place didn't make it a home. After my failed attempt to do it all on my own, my mom insisted that it would be a good idea if I joined the army. She didn't have to tell me twice. When I was eighteen, I joined up and left for basic training in Fort Jackson, South Carolina. I'm fairly sure my mother was ready for me to find my own home as long as it was out of hers.

Finally a Place Called Home

Fast forward about two years after I left, my mother is crying, frustrated, and sad. I can still hear her saying, "Now that I have finally gotten what I wanted, I feel like it's all being taken away from me." I came home on leave for a visit to support her during this terrible time, and I sat listening to her in her living room.

Being who she was, my mother had moved out of the apartment immediately after I had joined the military. In fact, she moved two more times: into a rental, and then soon after, she bought her very first home. Almost immediately after she bought the home, she started having some numbness in her thumb. We all thought it was a pinched nerve of some sort, but it turned out to be much worse. The doctors determined that she had terminal cancer of the brain and didn't have too much longer to live. The pain in her voice and that realization of seeming unfairness has been indelibly printed on my heart. After years of searching and finally finding home, eight months later, she was gone to her eternal home. For me, it may have been one of the pivotal moments of what led me to where I am today.

I spent twenty-one years in the military, calling many places home. If you've ever been in the military, or have known anyone that has, we have a common saying: "Home is where you hang your hat, cover, and beret [insert whatever head gear you like]." Home for me has been in places such as Kentucky, Hawaii, Georgia, California, Colorado, and yes, even the hot desert of Iraq, where I got to spend a wonderful year (yes, that's sarcasm) dodging mortars and saving lives as an army medic. Sometimes home wasn't so great, and sometimes home was a hard place to leave, but in all cases, home is where the army told me it was.

I'm not sure of the exact moment when I decided that the word home to me was more than just a word, but rather something from which I would create a ministry, so to speak. A friend and fellow church member told me, "You know, Brenda, what you do is your ministry." I never thought of what I do like that. Looking back over the years, I would have to say that finding home has been more of a lifelong journey for me, so it was probably inevitable that I would become a REALTOR®.

While growing up, not too many people think of a career choice as a REALTOR®. I don't remember one person saying, "I want to be a REALTOR® when I grow up." I don't believe I even knew it was

1 Word

an option until I bought my first home and found out that they existed. It was the combination of my life with my mother, my life in the army, and purchasing and selling homes through agents that made me gravitate toward this career. The work is really much more than a career choice for me. Just like the army, it is a way of life. Finding homes and helping others do so is a true passion for me (cue the eye roll—I know all realtors say that, but I truly mean it).

My home is now San Antonio, Texas. It's the final place I retired to after the army, and I decided to stay. It's truly home for me as my family, life, and passions are all right here, and I can say that, given my experiences and the journey that brought me to this point, I will never take it for granted. So that's a little bit about what home means to me. What does it mean for you? What thoughts, emotions, or experiences come to mind when you think of the word home?

Curves

AIMEE LANIER–CAMPER

The curves of your body do not define you. The curves of your life do not define you. It is how you handle those curves that helps shape who you are. Whether you are screeching around corners, kicking up dust and gravel behind you, slowly and gracefully meandering around curves, or taking your time to enjoy the scenery, it is all about how you handle yourself that builds your character. The ability to trust in grace and pull out of a skid before going off road tells a lot about you. Knowing when to make a U-turn before losing focus and getting off course keeps you true to yourself and helps you reach your destination.

1 Word

How Curves Shape You

The curves of tree trunks provide strength, helping trees reach for the sun and bud new life from their limbs, just as curves redesign your body's structure, empowering you to grow new life in your womb. Your curves make up your life force. They make you sensuous, voluptuous, and irresistible. The curves of your lips tell volumes about you, from a fleeting emotional response to the hint of deep secrets lying beneath the surface—a sly, crooked sneer or a warm, friendly smile. The curves of your aging face are a road map to your personal history that you try so hard to cover up, from frown lines or laugh lines to those crow's feet that show when you let your guard down and flash your biggest smile. The curves of your breasts, hips, and thighs, no matter what size, exude sexiness.

The curves of your belly, the curves you seem to spend the most time obsessing about, are at the core of your femininity. From weight loss to weight gain, these curves are constantly adapting. The miracle of your curves adapt to make room in your belly for a tiny, peanut-sized fetus you can barely see in that first ultrasound to grow into an eight-pound baby.

Aimee Lanier—Camper

Curves in the Road

Curves are a necessity in your life. At a time when many women focus on motherhood, I spent my mid-twenties and thirties focused on my career and the caretaking of aging family members. I soon would grieve the loss of both of my parents a few years apart. After a long-term relationship ended, the road to romance seemed to hit a roadblock. Any free time was devoted to volunteering in the community or at church. Then, my career path and responsibilities took a turn. Roads seemed to narrow, and I was hitting more and more roadblocks. I needed curves to get me out of the rut.

Curves always make your road trips more interesting. My dad, a lover of old, fast cars, had a sticker on his dash that said, "Get in, sit down, shut up, and hang on." When life throws me a curve, I often think about this phrase and the road trips I took with my mom and dad. We made many wrong turns along the way. We would laugh because, as Dad and I pointed out, Mom could read every speed limit sign we passed, but somehow she always misread the directional signage along the highway. We made U-turns, found country roads, discovered fun places to pit stop, and always enjoyed the adventures the curves of the road gave us.

1 Word

When you experience roadblocks, you can either allow yourself to get stuck on the side of the road, or you can get in, sit down, shut up, and hang on. In order to get unstuck, I chose to ride the curves. Like many women, by the age of forty, I had experienced grief, job loss, and relationship failures. Through faith, prayer, and listening for God's guidance, I learned to navigate the curves of life. I devoted time to worship and to do outreach work. I built a new career, worked my way up, and enjoyed promotions and a new fulfilling position. I decided to make time for myself and start dating, so once again, I was navigating the road to romance.

Never let your curves hold you back. As I began to put myself out there in the dating world again, the inevitable worry about my weight became an issue for me. Like many women, my weight had yo-yoed over the years, and too many times, I let the number on the scale determine what kind of day I was going to have. I was self-conscious at first, but I didn't let it hold me back, and I began to gain confidence. Though I was having trouble finding the right person for me, I wasn't having any trouble attracting dates. It seemed that the only person who had an issue with my weight was me.

Embrace Your Curves

Learn to love your body's curves. While it is certainly

important to strive for good health, you can still love your body as is. Making healthier food choices and getting more exercise helped me lose some weight, but I was still a "curvy girl." I learned to embrace that. I stopped being afraid to dress in clothes that showed off my curves. On this new adventure, I gained more and more confidence every day.

It's never too late to start enjoying the curves of life, so don't give up. From setups to online dates, one bad date after the other seemed to cause too may detours and distractions. Just when I was ready to put the car in park, I reluctantly accepted a lunch invitation from someone new, a racecar driver—someone who knows how to navigate the curves like a pro. Just like that, one little turn in the road, and guess what? I found the one. That one curve in the road I decided to take, that one date, started a whirlwind romance that would be the beginning of lots of wonderful adventures of twists and turns in the road. After a few short months, we were planning our wedding. We had so much in common. We had even both been told in the past that having children would not be likely for us, and this seemed to be just another thing we had in common. We were just fine with that, or so we thought, as we would have the freedom to travel and just enjoy each other.

I Word

You should always be ready to hang on around the hairpin turns you can't plan. Nothing could have prepared us for the next curve in the road. I got pregnant. I was over forty and pregnant. We were overjoyed and frightened at the same time. It was a risky pregnancy because of our ages, so we had many curves and ups and downs to navigate together. We went through months of tests and held our breath at each doctor's visit. We both had to shut up and hold on for our lives. We didn't tell anyone until we got test results back and knew we were going to have a healthy baby girl. We were thrilled to go public with our news. Something that was supposed to be impossible was indeed made possible. It was a curve only God could have created. We felt so incredibly blessed.

Your curves are powerful. As a first-time mom in my forties, I am in awe of the power of my body's curves and my ability to handle them as they change. Nobody really expected my pregnancy to go full term. We took everything month by month, week by week, and day by day. I was worried about my age and my weight, again. My wonderful doctor told me from the beginning that I wasn't her oldest, older-than-dirt patient, and she told me that I wasn't overweight and to stop worrying. I was very careful about what I ate. I drastically cut back on sugars and fats and avoided nitrates and caffeine. My body adapted for the new life growing inside me. I got curvier. Our baby girl grew. My husband rubbed my belly with cocoa butter every night as it continued to stretch. I got closer and closer to term.

Your curves nurture. Not only did my body carry a baby, but it carried a baby to term. The curves of my body did such a great job providing our baby with the space she needed in the womb that she had stretched out, gotten comfortable, and did not want to come out. We had a planned cesarean section delivery a few days before Christmas, and our daughter arrived. I had done it. I delivered a healthy baby girl. My family and I went home a few days later, and my body began to adapt again. I began the process of recovering from surgery while I learned to be a mom. Our baby enjoyed cuddling against my curves, feeling my body's warmth against hers.

Never let fear stop you from exploring a curve in the road. Even though curves can sometimes be stressful, they can certainly be rewarding. Like a lot of new moms, my maternity leave was both a wonderful and scary time. My husband and I had never even really been around kids before, much less taken care of a baby, so we had so much to learn, especially how to trust our instincts. I stressed about how I was going to balance family and career, and I had to work through changing hormones and mood swings. Everything suddenly seemed scary. I nested, trying to get comfortable in one place. I hit the brakes. I parked the car. It didn't take long for comfort to turn boring and depressing. I was going against my nature. I had to get back on the road, with a husband and baby along for the ride, and rely on faith. As I began embracing the curves again, my body healed along with my spirit. I began exploring a new, ever-changing curvy road.

Enjoy the Curves

The curves of life can take you places you never even dreamt about. Don't stay so focused on one path that you miss a curve that can take you above and beyond the destination you are shooting for. God always has a better plan in store for you. The curves God gave me took me quickly from a single, career-oriented woman to a married mother, learning to balance family life and work. I am blessed to wake up every morning to a loving husband and a beautiful baby girl. My home is filled with laughter and joy.

As we enjoy our newest journey, my husband tells me how much he loves his curvy girl. He still rubs lotion on my stretch marks, the marks that came from what was supposed to be impossible. I look at all the new curves of my body. I see all the curves, twists, and turns my life has taken. I embrace every curve and what it represents.

Our daughter, Amelia, is here now. We named her after Amelia Earhart because we want her to be adventurous and courageous; we want her to be a trailblazer and explore every curve in the road possible, and the curves that are impossible. I know she will navigate the curves of life like a champ. It's in her blood to get in, sit down, shut up, and hang on.

Examine Your Curves

How do you navigate the curves of your life? Do you handle them with grace or just speed through them? Do roadblocks cause you to stop your course, or do you find detours? Do you need a curve to come along to get you out of a rut? Who are your passengers as you go around the curves? How do your body's curves influence your journey? How do curves help you achieve your purpose? How will curves help you reach a destiny you haven't even dreamt of yet?

Stillness

DONNA T. BROWN

"Be still and know (recognize, understand) that I am God. I will be exalted among the nations! I will be exalted in the earth" (Psalms 46:10 AMP). This scripture has been a personal favorite of mine for well over twenty years now. It was given to me in the early days of my becoming a wife and mother. The benefits of knowing it have been quite rewarding, but the struggle to get there is an entirely different story. Stillness simply allows us to have calmness, tranquility, peace, and serenity. Being still may not be our entire makeup, but it is definitely a valuable characteristic needed to successfully function within our life's journey.

1 Word

Stillness: The Beginning

I was born and raised in a Mayberry-like town called Adamsville, which rests on the outskirts of Birmingham, Alabama. Growing up in Adamsville, I was fortunate to have a live-in grandmother who we affectionately called "Mama." Mama was our cook and our disciplinarian, and she would eventually be the connection between us and Jesus. In soldier formation, she would escort her then eight grandchildren a little less than a quarter of a mile to church each Sunday.

Children's Ministry was nonexistent, so we all nestled around Mama on the front pew to receive our godly orders for the week, but probably the only sermon my siblings and I clearly heard and understood would come from Mama's lips instead of the pastor's. She didn't ask, bargain, plea, or attempt to convince us to believe her. Her sentences were three very direct commands: "Hush chile," "Be quiet," and "Be still." Clearly, those were difficult requests for eight children to fathom, but because we were all too familiar with the consequences, we obliged her without question.

As I reflect on those times, I distinctly remember what I would gain by simply "being still." When I sat still, even for the few moments that I could, I had the opportunity to look around and capture the beauty of my surroundings. Things revealed themselves to me—things that I'd never noticed or cared to notice. As I sat still, I finally heard the words of those old Baptist hymns. And while I may not have fully understood the words of those songs, I knew in my heart that they were particularly meaningful to the congregants. I saw and felt the passion on the faces of those who participated.

When I sat still, I witnessed Mama's tears making a weary trek down her cheek, plopping onto the crinkled pages of her old Bible. This was preceded by my hearing muffled ramblings coming from her lips; ramblings that I would later understand to be prayers. This affected me deeply, and I was found that those things I came to notice prompted me to want to learn more. Again, it wasn't until I sat in stillness that those hidden treasures were revealed to me.

Another Level

As a blossoming teen, I needed to take stillness to another level. I was maturing much faster physically than I was mentally, and of course, that would offer greater provocation. It was during these years when I would be challenged by my peers to fit in and keep up with the latest trends. I was even asked to trade my innocence for popularity. This vulnerable

1 Word

chapter in my life yielded a flurry of situations that I wasn't emotionally responsible enough to handle. Some of which I passed with flying colors, and others, not so much.

Case in point, I was confronted by an extremely handsome, married suitor who was not only a familiar face in my family's circle, but he was also ten to twelve years my senior. He said all the right things a girl my age wanted to hear, especially from an experienced grown man. There were women his age who would have welcomed the opportunity. But hey, he chose me—the underage filly—as his vixen of choice. As much as I knew it wasn't right, my feelings of guilt were overtaken by the flattery. I was honored by his attention, and he was quite aware of that.

One day, he invited me to a secret location so we could "chat." Now, even my young and impressionable mind knew he wanted more, but I convinced myself that this would simply be innocent conversation. He made all the necessary arrangements for me to meet him. He applied a bit of pressure in his subtle invitation because he didn't want to allow me enough time to really think about what he was asking me to do. He didn't want me to ponder the thought of how it might affect me later, or the pain I would surely cause his wife by being her husband's young lover. Not to mention, she knew me, and she would have experienced great hurt by my betrayal, had she found out. However, in his planning, an unexpected distraction made its way into the picture. He received a phone call. A phone call that would offer me just enough time to be still and consider what I was about to do. It was at this moment that I allowed myself the opportunity to "be still" and consider the long-term repercussions that could erupt from this short-term encounter.

In my stillness, I began to reflect on everything my parents taught me about being a "good girl." And even though this invitation was flattering, I couldn't avoid feelings of endangerment. I acknowledged all of these things and decided against having our chat. It would be a decision that I am, to this day, so very thankful for. This wasn't the first, neither was it the last, of some hard choices I had to make while relying on my upbringing and the values Mama instilled in me. Again, some of the choices I made were great, and others, not so much.

As an adult, I find myself being prompted to hit the replay button on those tender childhood moments. I was an anxious, analytical, overthinking mess. I was filled with an unquenchable desire to act now and think later. When I was twenty-one, my childhood schoolmate and fellow church member pursued me. With great boldness and certainty, he shared with me that he asked God for a wife, and I was the one God showed him. His revelation was laughable for me because 1) I wasn't interested, 2) he was younger (although only a year and a half), and 3) I didn't date guys from my community.

Well, after eating crow, I would find out later on in our relationship that there was also a number 4: he was a "bad boy." He was extremely jealous and had anger management issues. What in the world had I gotten myself into? I knew I should have stuck to the code and turned down his advances, but I was in it now—deeply in it. I loved him. He would later propose, and I would accept. But the jealousy and insecurities didn't stop. In fact, they worsened. There would soon become a growing concern within my family and friends regarding my safety and wellbeing. Their feelings were definitely warranted because he didn't care who witnessed his erratic behavior, but I loved him and was torn.

Two weeks before our wedding, we had the biggest blow up in the history of our relationship. I ran outside into the darkness and screamed to the heavens for answers from God concerning this man. In the stillness of the night, I heard the voice of God speak to me: "Marry him." From that day until this one, I have never questioned what I heard. So amid family and friends' warnings and threats, and all other chaotic backlash, I stood on what I know I heard that night.

Two months after we were married, my husband was involved in a near-fatal accident. He was on his way to work early one morning and ran into the back of an 18-wheeler. When I arrived at the hospital, I was given an extremely dismal forecast for his life. The surgeon spoke candidly with me and shared that there was a 30 percent chance he wouldn't survive surgery. He had suffered severe head trauma, which had caused his brain to shift. Even if he survived surgery, he would live a pretty sad and unfruitful life. He would suffer from some pretty intense migraines and undergo long hours of both physical and occupational therapy. Last, but certainly not the least of his prognosis, the neurological damage would affect his ability to have children. This was hard, but for some strange reason, I was not moved. For several reasons, I was not myself that day. But the "self" that I'd become was so necessary in order for me to get through this ordeal. And as Moses challenged the children of Israel to "stand still and see the salvation of the Lord," twenty-six years and three children later, I have likewise watched the mighty hand of God move miraculously on my husband.

The Challenge of Being Still

Over the years, being still has served an amazing purpose in my life, yet it has been and still is somewhat of a personal challenge for me. Even today, it's an ongoing struggle for me to rest in stillness, but with each challenge, I make a conscious effort to resist those flesh-driven promptings. I wait for the flutter of the butterflies to settle, followed by a sweet ease that many of us can identify as peace. It's at that time, that I realize that I am right where I need to be to move forward. Being still might feel untouchable for you, especially if you lack discipline. I didn't value its importance until I allowed myself to reflect on how well it served me over the years.

I challenge you to practice it more often now than not. Upon doing so, you will find life to be much sweeter, awakened, and easier to deal with. Whenever you visit stillness, positive things will happen for you. You will hear, receive, ponder, and dream. You will be very present in your thoughts and not days or weeks ahead of yourself. Do not be alarmed if there's an ongoing battle within yourself that attempts to keep you from doing this as frequently as you should. Nevertheless, fight for the opportunity to be there because the rewards are invaluable. It is imperative. You need it in your life. It's a tranquil place that allows you to explore all the beautiful possibilities inside yourself.

When you practice stillness frequently, you will become a well-oiled vessel. Your attitude will be more pleasant and conversations more eloquent. You will find yourself choosing your battles with ease. Even your understanding will be greater, and you will process matters differently. Practicing stillness physically is even more intriguing. Your facial expressions will be more controlled, your countenance will change, and you will find yourself struggling less in your thought life. With age should come wisdom and self-control. Stillness ushers more of that to you. Its sweet interruptions will prevent you from making bad choices you would have otherwise made had you not rested in it.

It wasn't difficult for *stillness* to be my one word choice because it has been a constant rescue for me during difficult phases of my life. In it is a compilation of potluck treasures. Peacefulness, patience, rest, silence, and serenity are all the warm and fuzzy fillers that will help you live a more pleasurable life.

Believe

TIMEKIA BRAYBOY

Vision without action is merely a dream. Action without vision just passes the time. Vision with action can change the world.
—Joel A. Baker

Believe is defined as, "to think that something is true, correct, or real" (Cambridge Dictionary). To me, it means that all things are possible if you believe! The circumstances I go through are only temporary. When you have the understanding that there's always an end to every process, each circumstance you go through will get easier to overcome with time. Your life situations are almost like a computer: it outputs whatever the input commands. In essence, your beliefs, thoughts, and reactions to each circumstance determines the outcome and whether it will be a lesson learned or an earning from the lesson.

You must have faith in your abilities and confidence in the power to achieve all that you desire to manifest in your life. Your reality becomes the product of the belief you have within yourself. Because of the importance of your desired outcomes, it's imperative to intentionally sustain a positive mental attitude and the belief that you have the inner power to create my reality, despite the obstacles that may be in front of you.

If you believe that you can feel better, look better, think better, live better, and have better, you are right! You have the right to a life of abundance, if only you believe. It's a fact that life will happen, but you must mentally encourage yourself through continued belief in your dreams by hunting your goals daily and consistently taking action toward a worthy plan to achieve greatness for your life. Consistency is the key to the breakthrough.

In order to change your life, you must change your beliefs and thoughts, learn to speak your breakthrough into existence, and call forth the blessings in your life. Talk your way into receiving what you know you deserve. Then believe it, conceive it, and do what is necessary to achieve it, all while preparing to receive it. *In essence, you must believe, commit, and succeed.*

There was a specific time in my life where I had to put my belief to the test. My job had ended, I was entering into the process of being a single mom, and I humbly made the decision to reside with a relative until I was financially able to LIVE again. It wasn't an easy process to go through, but I was determined to have a successful outcome.

I recall arising daily, giving thanks to the Most High for going through this opportunity for growth, showing gratitude for nature and all the beautiful things he's created, and lastly, reflecting on my dreams while reviewing my goals to be achieved that day. My belief was so strong that I could see my now home before my eyes, I could touch the financial blessings with my hands, and I could see the smiles on my kids' faces. Had I given up on myself and focused on the situation (thus giving more power to it), I wouldn't be where I am today.

You must learn to live and embrace the opportunities that are good and not so good. You have the power to call forth poverty and wealth in your life through your belief and mental attitude. I often hear one of my mentors say, "You bring about what you think about." If you think you're broke, busted, and disgusted, more of that will be attracted to you. In the reverse, if you know you're wealthy, then wealth and riches will be attracted unto you. It's all a part of the law of attraction.

It's time to break the generational curses of self-doubt, disbelief, and discouragement to have and become greater. Through applying positive self-belief and a positive mental attitude, you will create a force to reckon with and witness your dreams becoming a reality. Don't allow others to make you feel guilty for believing you are rich and disassociating yourself from mediocrity. In order to have better, you must become better and surround yourself with people that have what you desire. Association brings similarity, so be careful of the company you keep. When your belief is producing gradual, desired results, take strides daily to become the change you wish to see in the world today. You are the only one that can make a difference.

Don't be afraid to believe in yourself. Be different, think differently, speak differently, and dream big! In the words of my mentor, Holton Buggs, "You must observe the masses and BE the opposite." Others may think you're out of your mind for the belief you have, but just remember that what a fool cannot learn to incorporate, he laughs at. Don't be content with being average. Average is learned, and above average is too.

When I was sleeping in a friend's basement on an air mattress, I never lost faith in myself. I went through that process to be a blessing to share with you that if I can believe greater and have more, so can you. You have what it takes to overcome any situation you may be enduring. It will not be an easy matter to implement belief, but you must completely accept your circumstances and continually take mental strides to victory.

You are born a winner with greatness inside of you. You are no longer a victim to the prison of disbelief. Allow your belief (mental attitude) to evolve, and no matter how you use it, you will get results. One of the main points to ponder is if whether or not this will work for you. The only way to demonstrate it is to try it yourself. I want you to brand in your mind that no matter how you implement belief in your mind, the results will follow. I believe in you, so NOW you must take action toward achieving the life only you know you deserve to have. Read this chapter reflectively and visualize a life of excellence to help you release your inner powers.

1 Word

In order to achieve a different outcome for your life, you must be willing to put in the work consistently in order to experience a life renewed. It is important to identify goals (one of which I'm sure is taking fearless action) and what's kept you from believing in yourself. Below are proven steps I've shared with multiple clients, and if done with consistent, persistent action, a positive mental attitude (no matter the circumstances), and full belief, you will achieve the desired outcomes in life.

1. Get a journal and write out your goals and dreams.

2. Meditate and pray (ask) about them.

3. Give your goals a timeline and commit them to memory daily (believe); while taking action, you will achieve them.

4. Have unstoppable, unbreakable, unshakable faith in that which you've taken action to achieve (receive).

At this point, I wish to indicate that in order to build up self-confidence and self-belief, you should be willing to affirm your life daily. If your mind has been obsessed with thinking patterns of insecurity or inadequacy, I want you to practice the power of self-talk. Get in the mirror and talk to yourself. Tell yourself over and over until you can feel it: **I believe in myself, I believe in myself, I believe in myself.** It may seem weird at first, but the more you practice it, the more you'll begin to feel it and believe it. Remember that your state of mental belief is reflected in not just your life, but your career, your health, your relationships, and even in your kids' lives.

Learn to think differently, fill your mind with positivity, and affirm the greatness about who you are created to be. Never think of yourself as a failure and never doubt reality, but embrace it, focusing on the desired outcome. Whenever a negative thought comes to mind, intentionally banish it by replacing it with words of empowerment. Do not create more difficulties for yourself through self-doubt and fear. Begin to think big; like the slogan of Nike, "Just do it."

Begin each day with a clear intention, and you'll be amazed at how quickly you manifest what you believe. Below are some positive affirmations to jumpstart the implementation of belief in your life:

- I believe in myself.
- I have faith in the Most High, myself, and my ability to achieve my goals.

I Word

- My thoughts create my reality.
- My belief enhances my life.
- My belief gives me identity and makes me who I am.
- I am becoming better everyday.
- I forgive myself for past mistakes.
- I have the power to manifest dreams.
- I serve people, and people serve me.
- I am worthy of positive relationships in my life.
- I create value in other people's lives.
- I am an outstanding success, and nothing can stop me.
- I treat every obstacle as an opportunity for growth.
- Money comes to me frequently and easily.

Know yourself and the power you possess. Read this chapter until it becomes a part of your daily life. You must remind yourself that God is with you, and nothing can defeat or harm you. Not to impose spiritual beliefs on you, but the Bible has a quote that I love the most: "All things are possible to him who believes" (Mark 9:23 NASB).

Impact

G. MICHELLE HALE

Oh, the power of one word! One positive word can move a person from merely existing to living, chaos to clarity, and aimlessness to aspiration. The one word that has had a profound effect in my life has been *impact*. This word has rekindled my passion and redirected my focus to make a difference in the lives of those I encounter along life's journey.

Every time I think of the word *impact,* it causes many emotions to surface in me. Gratitude and appreciation immediately come to mind because of the many good things that have happened in my life.

1 Word

I am truly grateful for all of the love, encouragement, and care that I have received from family and friends. When I reflect on encouragement given and kind deeds done to me by complete strangers, it gives me a reason to smile. When I consider the people that have made an impact on my life, the list is infinite, but due to time and space limitations, I will talk about a few people who have influenced my life the most.

Without a doubt, my grandmother, who raised me, has made the deepest earthly impact upon my life. Despite having only a third-grade education, she worked tirelessly to make sure that I would have a college education and learn to play the piano. My gratitude and appreciation for her unconditional love is bottomless. Next on the list would be my children—Carla, Melissa, and Michael Jr.—who are my greatest contributions to the human race. They have truly impacted my life and taught me some lessons in strength in the face of adversity, but that is a separate story for a different day. I have digressed enough, so now back to the word, impact.

A Revelatory Moment

I have heard impact being used for many years, and I often hear the phrases "making an impact" and "having an impact." Although I knew the meaning of the word, it would be years before I would discover how it applied to and gave purpose to my life. In November 2013, while attending the funeral service of a former teacher, this word took on a deeper meaning for me and has been a constant reminder of what is really important in life. Approximately fifteen minutes prior to the service, I was asked to give remarks as a former student. Without hesitation or reservation, I willingly consented. It was an honor to pay tribute to someone who had invested a great deal of time and genuine interest in my educational success. My task was easy because the memories of this teacher were permanently etched in my mind, crystal clear, and indestructible.

This experience provoked me to reflect on my past, present, and eventual mortality. I asked myself, am I making a positive impact upon anyone's life besides my family and friends? I then reflected on my daily living and various church and civic activities in which I was involved. Am I making an impact that displays strength, knowledge, dedication, and commitment? Are my motives genuine, or am I just building a resume and furthering my personal interests? Am I truly seeking to serve, or am I just seeking validation from others? Am I approachable? Do I exercise my gifts and graces to their maximum potential? Have I had such a profound influence on anyone's life that they could stand as I stood, unscripted, and speak confidently about me? This self-examination has helped me to channel my efforts to make a positive impact on the lives of others. As others have invested in me, I must invest in the lives of others. I have had to apply this word in many areas of my life.

Being a minister of music has provided me the opportunity to work with all ages; however, I have a passion for youth and children. Many of the youth and children that I have had in choir are now adults and productive citizens. Many have written me and stated that I had an impact upon their lives by showing interest in their lives beyond the choir. One once described me as a "champion for young people." Now that is quite an impact.

The Leading Example of an Impacted Life

There are many biblical illustrations of a person having an impact on another's life. One example is the relationship of Naomi and Ruth. Their relationship transcends racial and cultural backgrounds. The entire biblical account is found in the book of Ruth. It begins with Israelites, Elimelech, his wife Naomi, and their two sons relocating from Bethlehem-Judah to the country of Moab because of a famine.

Naomi's husband dies, and her sons marry Moabite women, Oprah and Ruth. Years later, the sons die, and Naomi is alone with Oprah and Ruth in a strange country. Oprah returns to her parents' home, but Ruth makes up her mind to stay with Naomi. Naomi's display of strength in the midst of tragedy and devastation to return to her homeland to rebuild her life made a lasting impact upon Ruth because Naomi was willing to leave her family and familiar surroundings to live and embrace a new land and way of life. Question to you: Besides family and friends, are you making a positive impact upon anyone's life?

Your Impact Starts Now

There are many ways we can make a positive impact that do not cost money. For example, giving someone a warm greeting, or perhaps asking, "How are you today?" These small acts of kindness can leave a lasting impression. You can make a positive impact by

Interacting – Becoming involved in community, civic, and church activities will give you an opportunity to connect and develop relationships with others.

Mentoring – Mentoring gives you opportunities to help develop and guide another's life. Share the knowledge of your past experiences to help others avoid pitfalls.

Preparing – Help others gain lifelong skills. Volunteer in areas where you are gifted.

Advocation – Everyone needs a person in their life who will celebrate their successes, sympathize with them during failure, and tell them the truth no matter how unpleasant. You can be an advocate for someone by always having their best interest at heart.

Communicating – We live in a time when technology allows us to communicate instantly. Texting, emailing, Facebook, etc., have provided platforms where we can stay connected. You can keep the lines open to dialogue.

Teaching – It is said that if you give a man a fish, he can eat for a day, but if you teach a man to fish, he can eat for a lifetime. You can make a positive impact by imparting the knowledge that you possess to strengthen others in the areas in which they struggle.

Be Mindful of Your Ability to Impact

One of the joys of my day is to send good morning texts to the contacts in my cell phone. The intent is not to see how many responses the texts generate, but to let the receiver know that someone is thinking of them and has taken the time to send a message. Some people respond; others do not. There have been times when I have been tempted to stop; however, it is at those times when I receive a message from one of my contacts saying that they appreciate the texts.

My point is that you should concentrate on making a difference in the lives of others. Remember, someone is always watching you, wanting to be just like you. Many times, the impact that you have on someone's life may never be realized until years later. The reality is that you will never know all of the lives you have influenced by your actions. Ask yourselves, who helped you? Who invested in you? Who imparted knowledge into you? You did not achieve all of your accomplishments on your own. Someone gave you an opportunity, which led to even greater opportunities to develop and expand on your success. Be grateful for the gifts that you have been given. "Every good and perfect gift is from above" (James 1:17 NIV).

All of my experiences have shown me not only that I can make an impact on the lives of others, but that I must make an impact on others because that is what I am called to do. I feel that it is one of the callings on my life. Just like playing the piano, it is a part of me. It is a passion that is inside of me. Making a lasting positive impact requires the ability and the desire to fuse. Without the fusion, it is only a learned behavior. There was a time in my life when my sister and I were taking piano lessons simultaneously. While she did learn to play several songs, she did not have a true desire to play the piano. Her true desire was to play the drums. There has to be something inside of you that motivates and drives you to continue to make a difference. The key is to find something (a cause) that you have the ability to do but also have the strong desire to accomplish. That drive cannot be predicated on the opinion of others.

I pose this question to you again: Besides family and friends, are you making a positive impact upon the lives of others? Just like with music, sometimes the greatest impact is realized after the music stops. Our impact upon others is often felt when we either leave a place or die, so I challenge you, just as I did the funeral audience in 2013, to begin today in making a positive impact on each person that you encounter.

Intentional

BRANDY BONNER

Repeat after me: I am an intentional woman (man). I am creator of my own life. I am creator of my dreams. I take intentional action toward living the life of my dreams every day. "I am" is the most powerful declaration that you can make. It is the name of God. You and I are made in the image of God; therefore, we are the fulfillment of our own words. If you don't believe me, just stop and take inventory of your life—the good, the bad, the exhilarating, the mundane. They're all created by your declaration and choice.

You're Late

I am coming straight in your face. As of this moment,

I Word

if you are not living out your full genius and experiencing health, wealth, and happiness in all things fabulous, you are behind! Yep, you're late! You say, "How am I late? You don't even know me!" You are late because you were born to thrive. You were born with everything you need inside of you to live an abundantly fulfilled life. You were born with a silver spoon in your mouth! I know you're ready to call me a liar and move on to the next chapter, but stay with me, please. I give you my word that over the next few minutes, I will show you how to revitalize your whole life. I will show you your silver spoon.

Before I go any further, let me take away another excuse you may have about why you may not be able to implement this tool of intentionality immediately in your life: your past. You may say I don't know how hard your life has been and all that you have had to suffer. You may say that I can't possibly imagine the severe trauma you experienced at the hands of your parents so early in life. You may say that I don't know how broken you really are, but I do.

The Highway to Intentionality

I am called the Dream Queen, but the startling contrast is that I had a nightmarish start. My childhood was so horrific that after escaping, I had to go on antidepressants to slow down the nightmares and process what had happened. I was afraid of everything. I pulled my hair out in balls. I crawled across the floor of my apartment so no one would see my shadow and want to come up and rape me. I attended a small group Bible study in college, where I sat in the closet with my sunglasses on. I was messed up! Until I took control of my life and became an intentional woman. There were several moments when I practiced intentionality, even though I didn't know what it was. I just knew it was life or death. No one was coming to save me.

At the age of seventeen, I packed a small bag and left my childhood home that was rattled with physical, sexual, emotional, and verbal abuse. I had the intent to live, not die. The night before I ran away from home, my mom told me she was going to kill me, so it really was a life or death situation. I didn't know why I had set my intentions on living, or if I had what it took to survive on the streets—if I had what it took to escape them. I recently heard that the most dangerous time for someone after escaping an abusive situation is the first six months. Six months? I didn't know if I would survive six minutes; they were coming to get me. That's a long time to be in danger on purpose. I didn't know the statistics. I was just intent on surviving. I would survive or die trying.

1 Word

Have you ever had those moments when it's "do or die"? Back up against the wall, you could lose everything, including your life? But you make up your mind and set the intention that you are going to take the risk. Come hell or high water, you will survive.

Put It in Perspective

The power of intention is like no other. Let's explore the definition of *intentional*. It means "done on purpose, deliberate, calculated, conscious, intended, meant, knowing, willful, purposeful, premeditated [I love that one], preplanned, preconceived" (Google).

I feel energized just writing this definition. My mind and my heart just expanded. How about you? Think for a minute about things you have done on purpose, whether it was finishing high school, going to college, coloring your hair, getting married to the love of your life or to your worst nightmare, having babies, or choosing your career. You did it all on purpose. Whether you are happy with your decisions or not, you must first admit that they are your decisions and then take full responsibility for them. You may be getting mad at me again, but stay with me. Help is on the way.

Let's go back to the definition of intentional and

explore a few of the words. I was shocked and intrigued to find the words "deliberate, calculated, premeditated, preconceived, and willful" as part of the definition. These words generally have negative connotations and are reserved for bad actions that someone does against another. These words are typically reserved for heinous crimes of robbery, rape, murder, etc. (He premeditated the murder of his wife. She willfully killed her children. He pre-calculated her every move before he snatched her up and raped her.) I know it's uncomfortable, but take a moment and feel the powerful emotions evoked by the fact that these crimes were committed intentionally.

The Power of Intentionality

Now, let us expand our consciousness. Let us take back the power of intentionality. What if we used that same power and same emotion to deliberately premeditate and calculate, with willful action, our dream life? Uh oh! Too soon? You can't even think about your dream life because you are still living a nightmare right now. Or at the very least, you are living a sad, brokedown, mundane, ritualistic, crappy life! No judgment from me—been there, done that, a thousand times.

You can change your life right now! Yes—right

now! It's as simple as setting an intention. You can start living a better, more stimulated, more aligned life right now through the power of intention.

Take control of your life by calculating, premeditating, and having a preconceived notion of the life you desire. Grab a piece of paper or a note card. Go ahead—I'll wait. On your paper, write down ten desires (loving relationships, money, home, business, weight loss, etc.) that you have for your life. Don't filter or hesitate. Just write. Don't stop and ask how. Just write. Don't make excuses for why it can't happen. Just write. Now write ten more and then ten more until you have a list of one hundred desires.

For many of you, this is the hardest assignment to complete because no one ever asks you what you want unless they are asking you what you want to eat. No wonder we are an overweight society—it's the only time anyone cares about what we want. Another reason is that your brain is trying to save you from pain and disappointment, so it immediately begins to tell you why you can't have what you want. It reminds you of past failures and that you couldn't possibly have the resources or the support to fulfill such desires.

Okay, now you have consciously, on purpose,

intentionally decided what you want in this life. Great job! You are on your way. You have just taken control and responsibility for your life. Congratulations! If you have not finished, please do so now. I will wait.

Now from your list, identify your top ten desires. Write them on a separate piece of paper. Write why you want these things. Why do you want them? How will having these desires met make you feel on the inside? (Yes, your feelings matter.) How will having these desires met change your current life? How will your life improve? What other doors will these desires lead to? Perhaps they will lead to a different job with fewer hours, time with family, travel, purpose? Please write down these answers.

Be the Example

You have now set an intentional, pre-calculated purpose for your desires. Boom! You are more powerful than any murderer because you are consciously using this power of intention for good. You have decided to better your life, and consequently, you are bettering the lives of those around you. We are all connected. When we start dreaming, those around us have permission to start dreaming too.

As I type this chapter, my husband is in his studio

(our basement) painting. See, after watching me and my daughter being at home, enjoying our life, going to school, and working on our businesses, he wanted a piece of the pie. He set an intention in his heart that at the right time, he would take a shot on his dreams too. He said we made dreaming look fun. It took his work truck to catch on fire to show him how short life really is. And he took the leap.

When we go after our dreams, we inspire those around us to do the same. When you feel fulfilled, your spouse, your kids, your friends, your coworkers, and your business partners are all elevated too. Whoa! You are now impacting the world just by intentionally setting the desires and purpose for your own life.

The Cost of Intentionality

The final step we will take in this chapter is to write down three intentional, calculated, premeditated, deliberate, willful acts you will take toward each of your ten desires. For example, if your desire is to be 150 pounds, your actions may be 1) buy new gym clothes, 2) enroll in a gym, and 3) find an accountability partner.

You now have thirty actions to take toward making your dreams come true. Those thirty actions become your daily to-do list. Pick one or two things to do toward your desires each day. Can you feel the power of this moment? You can live your dreams if you just do what is on this list! Now I got on my kick-ass life coach voice. Just do what the frick you say you gonna do. Plan your life and live it like you choose. Be intentional every frickin' day! Stop making excuses and take control over your own damn life. We all got pain! We all got shit to overcome! It's do or die for us all. It's survival of the fittest for all of the species on this planet. The ways of nature: only the strong survive, and the weak get left behind and eaten!

I'm passionate because I love people. I want you to live the fulfilling life you were destined to have. Abundance is your birthright. Yes, abundance is your birthright! Let's stop leaving our inheritance on the table. Let's decide what we truly desire and go after it in a premeditated, calculated way.

Start taking these actions toward your dreams right away. You and your life are going to change overnight. I didn't say you'd be rich overnight; I said you would be changed. And as you change and continuously take action, you will see your dreams come true one after another. Look fear in the face and say, "Get out of my way, I got shit to do!" Change your nightmares into your dream life by the stroke of your pen and the intention of your heart.

1 Word

That's all for now, but I hope you feel empowered. You will be hearing more from me. I am invested in seeing millions take rightful ownership of their lives and live the life of their dreams. Join me in living **the premeditated dream life.**

If you need me, don't hesitate to reach out to me. Be blessed.

The Intentional Woman

P.S: Do one thing that scares the shit out of you every day. This will keep your life fun and adventurous. One day, you'll look up and be living fearless. Imagine that.

Hope

CHARITA H. CADENHEAD

"*Every area of trouble gives out a ray of hope*"
—John Fitzgerald Kennedy

Well you've come a long way since the beginning of this *1 Word* journey. How are you feeling? Encouraged? Motivated? Either of the two will do, but in any case, I hope you are feeling different than you did before you began this road trip. Before we go, there is one last thing I'd like to share, and that's my thoughts on the word *hope*.

I don't always share my innermost thoughts, but this book dictates I do exactly that: share what's going on in my head. Not even those closest to me often get to hear what I'm thinking, so for now, let's just you and I talk. It may seem one sided at first, but at any time, you can stop and express your thoughts about something I've said. I promise it won't go any further than the space between these pages and your mind, unless you decide to share with someone else. Later, we're going to be talking specifically about you.

What Does Hope Mean to Me?

Let's keep it simple and start with my personal feelings about what hope means to me. Hope is a desire for a shift in a current situation that will lead to something better. That aspect of hope has never escaped me, but for a long time, I had only acknowledged the desire aspect of hope's definition. What I left on the table was the most essential part of what hope entails, and I didn't grasp it until I started this book project.

In the course of thinking about this book and my chapter, I realized that there seemed to have been a disconnect somewhere between things that I hope for and the actualization of those things. I had some idea that there was a missing link, but that link was nowhere on my radar. That is until I had a light bulb moment when I started writing about a decision that I made at church.

When I tell you about my light bulb moment, I already know that two of the most likely reactions will either be *duh,* or you'll find that your light bulb will start blinking in your head, just as it did in mine, thus your curiosity will be peaked. With any luck, you'll seek to rediscover the meaning of other words that you use without as much as a second thought.

Hope and the Disconnect

Remember I told you that I rediscovered the meaning of hope by accident, so for you to understand and really get it, let me tell you about the experience at church that shone a light on the disconnect that I had from hope's full meaning. That situation challenged me to rethink my stance on hope and come to a conclusion that was hard to admit.

When I joined my church several years ago, I attended a series of classes for new members, and on the last day of the class, we completed a spiritual gifts analysis so that we'd know which ministry we were best suited for. This analysis consisted of sixty questions and a choice of answers relating to how accurately the question or statement described the person completing the analysis—in this case, me. The points and answers ranged from -2 (N) not at all to +10 (M) most of the time. The scores were tallied up in twelve categories, **including prophecy,**

1 Word

service, teaching, exhorting, sharing, leading, mercy, love, enthusiasm, prayer, and of course, hope.

I don't remember what I originally scored, but a couple of years later, I took the survey again because I had not found where I could best serve in the church, and I was eager to find a place. Much to my surprise, on a scale of 1 to 10 (10 being the highest score), I scored a 3 on hope. I thought, how could this be? There isn't a day that goes by that I don't think about hope. Even if I'm not focusing specifically on something desirable, the word itself enters my mind and just stays there for a while. It's as if it has come to my psyche to rest, relax, or to otherwise just chill for a time. My mind becomes a hammock or chaise lounge for hope. It's almost as if hope knows that I need time to chill because thinking about the word puts me in a relaxed state of mind, and that's a really big deal for me because my mind never shuts down from the clutter which is my life; that is, until hope shows up.

Immediately after calculating my score, I thought, there has to be a mistake. Maybe I had added up the points incorrectly or perhaps inadvertently marked the wrong answers for some of the questions. So I took the survey again, and my score for hope was the same: 3. My shoulders slumped in disappointment. It saddened me to think that I had mistaken hope for something else, but what? Pondering for only a few minutes, I rationalized how the survey could have interpreted hope so far down on the scale.

Listen and follow carefully so that I don't lose you. Before you can even try to conceive my rationale, you need to know the following about me. According to 16Personalities.com, which is a website that profiles the sixteen personality types (eight extrovert personalities and eight introvert personalities), I am a "great analyst and abstract thinker," and I "view the world as a big, complex machine, and recognize that as with any machine, all parts are interrelated. INTPs excel in analyzing these connections, seeing how seemingly unrelated factors tie in with each other in ways that bewilder most other personality types."

You're probably saying, huh? What the heck does all of that mean? It means that I view hope, much like everything else, as a complex idea—one that simply cannot be responded to without assessing situations. When I took the survey, I would say that the vast majority of my answers were the result of the imagery of specific situations, which may apply to a particular question. I didn't think long and hard about it; the images or situations just popped into my head when I read the question, and I answered according to the situation. I deduced that I couldn't answer the questions in the abstract. The only way that I could answer the question was to relate it to a specific situation. In other words, I analyzed it by breaking it down and tying it to a specific situation where hope was involved.

I used to wish that I could answer the questions in general terms. I had concluded that that must be the reason I scored so low in the category of hope. The question of why continued to plague me. I'm a little obsessive in that I don't like unanswered questions, and I don't like not fully understanding something. As I continued my search for a reasonable rationale, the light bulb finally came on.

The Light Bulb Moment

The light bulb finally lit up when I looked up the word hope in the dictionary. Low and behold, the disconnection slapped me right in the face. Check this out. The Oxford English Dictionary offers this definition: "to entertain expectation of something desired; to look (mentally) with expectation; expectation of something desired; desire combined with expectation." Merriam-Webster Dictionary adds that "hope implies little certainty but suggests confidence or assurance in the possibility that what one desires or longs for will happen."

Did you catch it? Do you see what I had been missing in my perception of hope? It was the expectation and anticipation. In that moment of clarity, that low score that I got on the spiritual gift analysis had me pegged. I can't tell you how hard that was to admit to myself. But I can tell you this: without that acknowledgement, there wasn't going to be a chance in hell that I would ever fully benefit from the seeds that I sow. No matter how strong my desire is, it does not and will not constitute hope if I don't associate and approach it with anticipation and expectation.

While I had the desire aspect of hope down pat, hope was often sabotaged by my lack of expectation and anticipation. In order for hope to even exist, there has to be desire and expectation. See, I told you it was going to be a duh moment, but so be it. Oh and in case you're wondering, I scored highest on the following: leading, 10; exhorting (strongly encourage or urge) and enthusiasm, 9. These words have now been added to my list of words to examine their impact in my life. This experience exemplifies the reason for this book for several reasons:

1. Because of the way we use words, we often lose sight of their actual meaning.

1 Word

2. We are directly affected by the words that we use by choice or chance.

3. We have to be careful what we say, how we say it, and to whom we say it to (including yourself).

4. The words you speak have a way of shaping your perspective, distorting your reality, and causing you to accept a lie as the honest-to-God's truth.

The Science of Hope

Before we part ways, let's look at hope from the perspective of science and change. I read an article in *Spirit Science* journal by Dr. Andrew Newberg, a neuroscientist at Thomas Jefferson University, titled "Speak with Love: How Your Words Literally Restructure Your Brain." In this article, he said, "A single word has the power to influence the expression of genes that regulate physical and emotional stress." I don't know if that's really a newsflash, but I totally accept that as truth and can appreciate any reminder that words, and the manner in which we think about them, absolutely matter and can alter our behavior.

When I am fully absorbed in a state of hope, I get genuinely excited about things that I'm hopeful for. I get this sensation of chills running up and down my arms. I can actually feel myself shivering for an instant. It's not a bizarre feeling, but rather it's almost like thinking about the magnificence of God. Like knowing that God is so great and so awesome that I can hardly fathom how great He really is. I almost have to stop thinking about it just to catch my breath. After regaining my breath, the sense of excitement transitions to a sense of calm that comes over me, and all I want to do at that moment is soak it up like a sponge soaks up water. Yep, Dr. Newberg and I are eyeball to eyeball on the power of a single word and the ability of words to alter our physical and emotional state.

You have to experience it for yourself and to explore things that make you feel that way. What words or things heighten your senses in such a way that there is an immediate and gratifying high of sorts and then a tremendous sense of calm? Before you get too caught up in that thought, let's just rule out that I'm referring to sex, okay? Hey, I had to kick that in there because as I was typing, my mind suddenly presumed that my question would send you there.

I can't help but wonder why some people don't harness control of their words more often than they do. Even now, I wonder if you will stop for a minute and contemplate how you can take more control of your thoughts. I wonder if you will be more intentional about your word choices, including the all-too-important and often misapplied self-deprecating self-talk. With any hope, self-deprecation will convert to self-appreciation. It may require some practice, but it can be achieved, and every effort should be made to reach that goal.

Nothing Is Unchangeable

I want you to engrave in your brain this quote by President John Fitzgerald Kennedy during his 1962 State of the Union Address: "Every area of trouble gives out a ray of hope; and the one unchangeable certainty is that nothing is certain or unchangeable." Nothing is unchangeable. How powerful is that? Like the word hope itself, President Kennedy's words send chills through my body.

The mere thought that the potential for hope to become a reality is at your disposal. Your mind should be recollecting all of the matters that you've cast aside because you believed that there was nothing you could do. Your mind should be running ahead of the race, knowing that every situation can be changed or modified in some way for the better. One question should be surfacing right about now: how do you find hope in situations where it seems unfathomable? Like anything that's been lost, if there is ever any hope of finding it, you have to first look for it. So is the case for hope.

Final Words

When you think about God and faith in our Lord and Savior, you need hope to believe in the very essence of faith. Whether one consciously thinks about hope or not, it's impossible to flourish without it. Reverend Jesse Jackson had it right in the sixties when he coined the phrase, "Keep hope alive." It was relevant then, and it's even more relevant today.

I want you to allow yourself the pleasure of expectation and anticipation that what you hope for is going to happen. Hope is not wishful thinking; rather it is backed by the certainty that nothing is definite in this world, but that's no reason to discount the viability of the thing hoped for.

You've heard of and may have experienced anticipatory anxiety caused by working yourself into a state of panic over something bad that might happen. How about implementing anticipatory actuality or anticipatory realization whereby you anticipate the best possible outcome? That is what you would call hope in action or in full swing.

I Word

Allow yourself to breathe deeply yet excitedly by the thought of the desired outcome.

You're probably asking yourself right now, but what if I do that, and I work myself up so much that when it doesn't happen, I'm gravely disappointed? I would ask that you stop it right now. Don't let that negative thinking deprive you of hope. Don't ever let anything or anyone, especially you, rob you of hope.

All this talk about hope and yet the one thing about it that I managed to miss was the anticipation that what I hoped for would actually come to pass. My long lost friend, the dictionary, slapped me in the face and raised my level of consciousness.

Words matter. Word choices matter even more. Choose your words carefully when talking to yourself as well as speaking to others. Listen to words that keep resurfacing in your mind, and make certain that you understand what they mean. Even if you think you understand, double check just to make sure. You may be surprised that you don't know at all. If you remember nothing else from this chapter, remember that desire alone does not constitute hope; it's a combination deal: desire plus expectation equals hope. Continue to hope, and never forget that without anticipation or expectation, it's just a wish.

Well, my job is done here for now. As you think about hope, its place, and its extraordinary meaning in your life, attitude, and actions, ask yourself this: how does hope influence your life and the life of those that cross your path? This isn't a rhetorical question, and it's not as easy to answer as you may think. So take your time. No pressure.

I fully anticipate that you'll be able to answer the questions in this chapter and this book from an entirely new perspective and awaken your mind to receive not only new information but also the possibility of new information.

1 Word Book II

Once authors started signing up to be a part of the *1 Word* book, I immediately knew that *1 Word* book II would follow. Having said that, if you have taken an interactive part in reading this book by soul searching and truthfully and candidly answering the questions posed, then you very well may already have the makings of a chapter in the second book.

If you would like to be considered as a coauthor for book II, please refer to the *1 Word* book guidelines (subject to change for Book II) at:

http://1WordBook.com and then email me, Charita H. Cadenhead, at renewrefreshreset@gmail.com and tell me the following:

- How did you hear about the *1 Word* book?

- What would be your one word for Book II?

- Why you would like to be a part of the project?

- How would your chapter benefit readers?

Please note that you do not have to be a writer or author to participate in the project. All you have to have is the desire to be one. Even if you've only written in a journal and haven't written anything publicly, you can become a part of the next *1 Word* book.

Your 1 Word Journal

You have had quite a lot to consider while reading this book. All of us authors ask you some very poignant questions. Make no mistake about it—the questions are not rhetorical. They are designed to serve a real purpose and add real value to your life, or as Sabrina Mays put it, we want you to Be Resilient, Add Value Everyday.

Please use these blank pages to put it all together. Not only will you give consideration to some things you haven't thought about for a while, but you may awaken the writer in you, and there is nothing more rewarding than putting pen to paper for the sake of clarity.

Happy Journaling,

Charita H. Cadenhead

1 Word

First, make a list of words that you believe have played a significant role in your life. Then, narrow the list down to a single word that resonates with you most.

_____

_____

_____

_____

_____

_____

_____

_____

_____

_____

_____

_____

_____

_____

Your 1 Word Journal

My one word is:

_____

What does the word mean to you?

_____

_____

_____

_____

_____

_____

_____

_____

_____

_____

_____

_____

_____

_____

_____

1 Word

How does the word make you feel?

_____
_____
_____
_____
_____
_____
_____
_____
_____
_____
_____
_____
_____
_____

Your 1 Word Journal

What was a turning point when you had to apply this word to your specific situation?

_____

_____

_____

_____

_____

_____

_____

_____

_____

_____

_____

_____

_____

_____

_____

_____

1 Word

How did or does the word move you from where you were into how it serves you now?

_____

_____

_____

_____

_____

_____

_____

_____

_____

_____

_____

_____

_____

_____

_____

_____

_____

Your 1 Word Journal

Feel free to use this space to write and reflect on each author's questions throughout the book.

1 Word

◈ ABOUT THE AUTHORS ◈

Sreelatha Meleth is a senior research statistician and works for an international non-profit organization. She has an eclectic education: a bachelor's degree in mathematics and physics, a master's in English literature, a second master's in community health and epidemiology, a third master's in applied statistics, and a doctoral degree in applied statistics. In addition, she is a certified adult educator and teacher of English as a second language.

She has lived in the Middle East, Great Britain, and Canada and is now a naturalized citizen of the United States. She has written over sixty-five scientific publications, and she has also written several published short stories and non-fiction pieces in the *Immigrant Women's Journal* in Saskatoon, Saskatchewan. Some of her short pieces were used as teacher's aides for multi-cultural education by the education department in Saskatoon.

She is the creator of the blog "In My Meditation Today" and soon hopes to publish a memoir in the next couple of years as well as publish some of her children's stories.

1 Word

Carole Hines-Sharp is a wife, mother of four adult children, grandmother to eight grandchildren, and survivor of triple negative breast cancer. She was born and raised in Birmingham, Alabama, and now happily resides in Rialto, California.

Carole has had two highly unexpected experiences in her life that will forever change her. The first is having survived breast cancer. Because of that life changing experience, she now holds the designation of cancer survivor that so many hold with honor and dignity. As a survivor, she now helps others navigate through the uncertainty of this deadly disease and helps them cope through it all.

Carole can be reached at cdsharp11@gmail.com, and she will gladly talk to and help anyone through the trauma that follows the words, "You have cancer."

About The Authors

D. Green Joseph discovered the love of writing in high school and has been inspired to convey humor, encouragement, and life experiences through the written word ever since. Joseph is currently a blogger on Renew Refresh Reset Your Life and LinkedIn, and she was a contributing writer for *The Faith Connection and Pure Heart* magazines. She is often called upon to compose and edit resumes, cover letters, speeches, and consumer/administrative correspondences.

She is a native Washingtonian (DC) now living in Birmingham, Alabama, and is the managing partner of Let's Go Solutions, LLC. Joseph graduated from Clark Atlanta University with a degree in journalism and has one daughter.

Her other passions involve giving back to the community through the Coach Reginald S. Joseph Memorial Scholarship, Women Under Construction, At Home with Shellie Foundation, and other nonprofits and church ministries.

Email:
Spaceinnovations2@gmail.com or d21joseph@ gmail.com

LinkedIn: Let's Go Solutions – D. G. Joseph

1 Word

Sabrina Mays is a Birmingham native and mother of two. She earned a BS in justice sciences from the University of Alabama at Birmingham and an MBA in human resource management from American Intercontinental University.

She is a community activist and serves as a board member for Brave, Inc., the Birmingham Public Library Young Professionals Board, Latch and Live Foundation, Traveler's Aid of Greater Birmingham, and Beyond Boundaries, LLC.

In 2011, Sabrina founded BRAVE, Inc., a nonprofit that serves low-income seniors and children by providing creative opportunities to improve their quality of life through healthy initiatives, physical fitness, and nutrition education.

In her free time, she enjoys hiking, walking, exploring the city, and serving the community.

Email:
yourebrave@gmail.com;
info@yourebrave.org

Facebook: You're Brave

About The Authors

Patricia A. Campbell is the author of the devotional, *Pocket Inspiration: 31 Days of Inspiration,* a prolific teacher, conference speaker, intercessor, prayer warrior, and minister of the gospel. She is the founder of Life Ministries, a ministry whose assignment is to empower the body of Christ to live in fullness and excellence. She is a woman of God, in touch with the pulse of the Spirit.

In addition, Patricia is an inspirational coach, mentor, and business consultant. Patricia enjoys spending time with her daughter, April, her granddaughter, Shriya, her son-in-law, Herbert, and her extended family. She also enjoys writing, reading, bowling, and traveling.

Email:
Ministerlife@aol.com

Twitter: @ministerpatric2

Lupe Moreno is the founder of Building Resilience and Strength. She is a certified life coach, resilience instructor, speaker, and domestic violence advocate. She is the author of *Unmasking the Silent Killer: The Many Faces of Domestic Violence* and is currently working on her memoir.

After more than twenty years as a domestic violence victim, Lupe Moreno found herself struggling as a single mother with three children. Like other survivors of domestic violence, Lupe lacked self-esteem, confidence, and self-worth. It was her faith in God that gave her strength to go on. Her faith also gave her hope in finding true love.

Lupe is now happily married to her soul mate and has the life she once only dreamed of living. Because of her faith, Lupe's life is now barely recognizable from the young girl who once lived daily in fear.

Email:
resilienceandstrength@aol.com

www.resilienceandstrength.com

About The Authors

Hermione Alease Carnes is chef (chief hospitality engineer for fabulous events) and owner of Elijah's House of Food Services, LLC, DBA Alease's Edibles. She began her catering service in 2001 in Fairfield, Alabama. She has worked as a chef instructor, personal chef, pastry and baking service contractor, and pop-up restaurateur. She obtained a bachelor's of science in accounting from the University of Alabama at Birmingham and an associate of arts from Culinard at Virginia College.

Hermione believes that all of her gifts, including training and writing, have enabled her to touch lives that she never would have encountered. Her clients range from the stranger at a homeless shelter to film stars, and everyone in between. She seeks to become a well-known brand that uses food, faith, love, and the skill of culinary arts to touch people in every area of life possible. She has one son, Seth William, who inspires her to keep going, never give up, and always pray.

Website:
www.aleasesedibles.com

Facebook: Alease's Edibles
Twitter: @hermionealease

1 Word

Brenda Mullen is a wife, mother, award-winning realtor, retired army medic, and lover of cats. She is currently a broker-associate for RE/MAX Access, serving the greater San Antonio, Texas, area and has been helping people find homes for nine years.

Brenda is living her true calling. Her deepest joy is when she helps a first-time or millionth-time buyer find that perfect place. It gives her some of the greatest satisfaction to help sellers sell their first home, or their second or third homes, so that they can continue their journey to find their sanctuary. If you need to reach out to Brenda, you can go to her websites at

Email:
brenda.mullen@sbcglobal.net

www.schertztxhomes.com and
www.findurwayhome.com.

About The Authors

Aimee Camper was raised in Fairfield, Alabama, and currently resides in Hueytown, Alabama. Her background is in natural health, herbology, and the mind, body, spirit connection. She holds a bachelor's of arts in American studies from the University of Alabama. Her hobbies include photography and writing. She is also a classic car enthusiast and uses the hobby as a method of community outreach for volunteering and fundraising for local charities. She is actively involved in serving her community through her neighborhood association, classic car club, and church.

Aimee has been published in the *Holistic Times Newsletter, Comprehensive Iridology Newsletter, Biodiversity Magazine,* and the Renew Refresh Reset Your Life Blog. She currently displays her involvement with her non-profit volunteerism from her work for the city of Homewood, serving the city council and mayor. Aimee and her husband, Barret, recently experienced the birth of their first child, Amelia.

Email:
aimee13@charter.net

Facebook: Aimee Lanier Camper

Donna T. Brown is a licensed and ordained minister. She's a realist who strongly believes her adversities help her to help others. She is the founder of Sisters SOS (Saving our Sanity), a support group that encourages women to confront their personal demons.

Donna is a teacher and speaker. She enjoys writing poetry and has written two songs for a local recording artist. Donna is also a comedian, and in October 2015, she placed second in *America's Funniest Home Videos*. Her videos and comedy sketches can be seen on You Tube and her personal Facebook page. She also does stand-up, featuring lighthearted church humor.

Donna is the wife of Jimmy L. Brown Sr., and the mother of Teryl, Jimmy, and Autumn. She makes her home in Trussville, Alabama.

Email:
jimmyanddonna@charter.net

Facebook: Donna N Jimmy &
It's Okay to Laugh in Church
Twitter: ItsOk2Laff

About The Authors

Timekia R. Brayboy, army veteran, inspirer, speaker, and life strategist, was born and raised in Birmingham, Alabama. This inspiring woman has the drive and burning desire to be the change she wishes to see in the world today. She exemplifies the characteristics of an influential leader and has earned multiple awards and recognitions, to include the Joint Service Commendation Medal for outstanding leadership from the Secretary of Defense of the United States of America.

This ambitious leader paints a unique illustration to visualize excellence from within. Timekia has a gift to empower individuals to open the box of imagination.

Timekia is celebrated as a source of inspiration and master motivator, empowering others to live life intentionally while believing in themselves. "Freedom Coach" describes her gift to influence audiences to break free from the destitute circumstances in their lives.

LinkedIn and Facebook: timekiabrayboy
Instagram: @coachtbrayboy
Twitter: @tbrayboy

1 Word

G. Michelle Hale is currently a minister of music at St. Thomas UMC in Sylacauga, Alabama. She is an avid reader and emerging writer who has published articles in *The Christian Index,* the official publication of the Christian Methodist Episcopal Church, and *The New Beginnings Newsletter,* the official publication of the North Alabama Southeast District United Methodist Women. She is a member of the Central Alabama Writer's Guild Alliance (CAWGA), and she is currently submitting articles for publication.

When she isn't glued to a computer screen, Ms. Hale spends time volunteering, participating in and supporting church activities, attending music functions, and socializing with friends. She is a proud mother of three children, Carla Michelle Hale-Marshall, Melissa Ann Hale, and Michael Carr Hale Jr., and G. G. to granddaughters Adrienne and Kennadi.

Email:
gmhale@gmail.com

Facebook: G. Michelle Hale

About The Authors

Brandy Bonner is an author, speaker, and coach. She is a California native, but has spent her life in Kansas City, Missouri. Brandy is known as the "tell-it-like-it-is Dream Queen." She helps people reframe their past, rediscover their dreams, and execute their dream life with intention. She is sought after for being raw, real, and point blankly telling her truth. Brandy is a regular contributor for the *Huffington Post,* as well as various blogs and podcasts. She is currently working to release her memoir next year.

Brandy is an avid reader, a student of personal development, and a master manifestor. She enjoys spending time with her husband and her daughter, whom she home schools. They enjoy learning, dancing, laughing, and exploring the ways of the universe together.

Email:
bbonnerconsults@gmail.com

www.milesinminutesconsultant.weebly.com
www. consultbrandyb.com

Charita H. Cadenhead is the visionary author who gave birth to the idea of this book. She is a mother to one daughter and a grandmother of two. She is a licensed Realtor® in the state of Alabama. In addition, she is the creator of the Renew Refresh Reset Your Life blog and the host of the Renew Refresh Reset Your Life TV podcast on Firetalk, where she interviews people who have made significant changes in their lives.

Charita is an author with three books, including an Amazon #1 Bestseller, to her credit: *Sell Your House Fast for the Right Price*, *I Am Woman: 21 Triumphant Women Sharing Their Journey to Embracing Truth and Their Authentic Self*, and of course, *1 Word*.

Charita has a particular interest in comfort zones—why people stay trapped in them and how they exit out of them. She knows all too well what it's like to be trapped in that zone, and she understands that breaking out of the zone often requires strategic planning.

Email:
RenewRefreshReset@gmail.com

www.RenewRefreshReset.com

LinkedIn: chcadenhead

SOURCES

Scriptures marked AMP are taken from the Amplified Version®. Copyright © 2015 by The Lockman Foundation. All rights reserved.

Scriptures marked ESV are taken from English Standard Version®. Copyright © 2001 by Crossway, a publishing ministry of Good News Publishers. All rights reserved.

Scriptures marked NASB are taken from the New American Standard Bible®. Copyright © 1960, 1962, 1963, 1968, 1971, 1972, 1973, 1975, 1977, 1995 by The Lockman Foundation. Used by permission.

Scriptures marked NIV are taken from the New International Version®. Copyright © 1973, 1978, 1984, 2011 by Biblica, Inc.™. All rights reserved.

Scriptures marked NKJV are taken from the New King James Version®. Copyright © 1982 by Thomas Nelson. All rights reserved.

Scriptures marked NLT are taken from the New Living Translation®. Copyright © 1996, 2004, 2007, 2013 by Tyndale House Foundation. All rights reserved.

Unless otherwise indicated, scripture quotations are from the Holy Bible, King James Version. All rights reserved.

WE WANT TO HEAR FROM YOU!!!

If this book has made a difference in your life Charita would be delighted to hear about it.

LEAVE A REVIEW ON AMAZON.COM!

BOOK CHARITA TO SPEAK AT YOUR NEXT EVENT!

Send an email to:
booking@ publishyourgift.com

FOLLOW CHARITA ON SOCIAL MEDIA

f Charita Hughley Cadenhead

🐦 @chcadenhead

"EMPOWERING YOU TO IMPACT GENERATIONS"
WWW.PUBLISHYOURGIFT.COM

www.ingramcontent.com/pod-product-compliance
Lightning Source LLC
Chambersburg PA
CBHW071622080526
44588CB00010B/1225